The Marine Insurance Handbook

THE MARINE INSURANCE HANDBOOK

AN EXPLORATION AND IN-DEPTH STUDY OF MARINE INSURANCE LAW AND CLAUSES

Bahaeddin Saffarini (ACII)

© 2016 Bahaeddin Saffarini (ACII)
All rights reserved.

ISBN-13: 9781533497338
ISBN-10: 1533497338
Library of Congress Control Number: 2016912169
CreateSpace Independent Publishing Platform
North Charleston, South Carolina

Table of Contents

Acknowledgments · vii

Preface · ix

Chapter 1   Cargo Clauses · 1

Chapter 2   War and SRCC · 21

Chapter 3   Institute Cargo Clauses 2009 · · · · · · · · · · · · · · · · · · 27

Chapter 4   Institute Clauses for Particular Commodities · · · · · · · · 46

Chapter 5   Institute Time Clauses—Hulls, January 10, 1983 · · · · · · 56

Chapter 6   Institute Time Clauses—Hulls: Restricted Conditions · · 77

Chapter 7   Reinsurance · 88

Chapter 8   General Average · 95

Chapter 9   The Marine Insurance Act of 1906 · · · · · · · · · · · · · · 107

Chapter 10   International Conventions · · · · · · · · · · · · · · · · · · · 184

Chapter 11   Protection and Indemnity Associations (P&I Clubs) ·· 196

Chapter 12   Incoterms 2010 Rules ······················· 201

Chapter 13   Letters of Credit ··························· 208

Chapter 14   Fraud ································· 217

Chapter 15   The Ships ······························ 223

Chapter 16   Cargoes································· 243

References ····························· 273

ACKNOWLEDGMENTS

For many years, I dreamed of writing a book on marine insurance that could benefit newcomers to the insurance market as well as the marine and nonmarine insurance practitioners who look for various references to assist them in their daily work or to develop their knowledge in this specialized field.

To be forced to retire after forty-four years of employment in the insurance sector was a real frustration, but we are all humans and should recognize the fact that there is an end to everything.

With encouragement and support from my wife, Hanan, my son, Watheq, and my two daughters, Maram and Aseel (who created the appropriate atmosphere for me to spend at least two hours a day writing this book for more than four months), I achieved my goal of writing this book in spite of limited financial and material resources.

I hope that the contents are beneficial and interesting for those who plan to become insurance professionals with careers based in international insurance law and practice.

PREFACE

The idea for this book came in response to the demand by various interested insurance professionals, as well as local institutes and insurance companies, to have one reference containing the necessary information aimed at developing and improving the skills and knowledge of newcomers to the insurance industry.

The book, although titled *The Marine Insurance Handbook*, contains the guidelines that marine underwriters or claim managers use to make their decisions on daily, practical cases based on established legal rules and decisions. It also contains the most internationally applied insurance clauses issued by the Institute of Marine Underwriters and the Lloyd's market, which are universally accepted and are either based on legal cases or market agreement.

This book contains collections of the various Institute Cargo Clauses with a comparison between the 1982 and 2009 editions as well as the Institute Time Clauses—Hulls and related clauses for insurance on ships.

Brief articles on the well-known terms of the International Chamber of Commerce (Incoterms) are included as relative issues to cargo underwriting. The subjects of fraud, letters of credit (L/C), the relations between banks and insurers, and protection and indemnity clubs are also added, as they are considered necessary for underwriters or claims managers.

Details on the various types of ships and carried cargoes are also given with attention to the major commodities carried by sea. International conventions covering international laws governing the carriage of goods by sea, land, and air are included, as they are of importance to underwriters as well as to marine claim handlers.

The subject of reinsurance is addressed, with attention to the major types of treaties used in the market by small and medium insurance companies. A summary on General Average and York-Antwerp rules has been added for necessary reference, but details were left for the licensed loss adjusters.

The Marine Insurance Act of 1906 is given special attention, as it is considered the main legal and practical reference for marine insurers in particular and other insurance professionals in general.

Bahaeddin Saffarini (ACII)

CHAPTER 1

CARGO CLAUSES

In November of 1978, The Secretariat of the United Nations Conference on Trade and Development (UNCTAD) distributed a document entitled "Marine Insurance—Legal and Documentary Aspects of the Marine Insurance Contract."

The Secretariat found that "the entire marine insurance industry had evolved historically from, and had largely retained practices and conditions of cover," which were formulated by insurers from developed countries. It had recognized the United Kingdom as the "international market center of marine insurance." The Lloyd's form of policy (the SG form) and many of the clauses used at the time of issuance of the report were criticized as antiquated and liable to be misunderstood. Accordingly, as UNCTAD is an intergovernmental body, representatives of the British insurance industry were invited to give their views, and the process of consultation began, in spite of the criticism from Lloyd's representatives and London underwriters of the interference with the smooth running of the market.

However, with an aim for reform, Lloyd's Underwriters' Association and the Institute of London Underwriters set up a joint working party. The move aimed at considering what might be done to counter the criticism made in the UNCTAD report and to drag the standard policy forms into the twentieth century.

In fact, the review of the policy conditions is one of the responsibilities exercised at all times by the Joint Cargo Committee and the Joint Hull Committee. When there are proposals to amend or update any of the standard forms, the drafting is undertaken by yet another joint committee called the Technical and Clauses Committee.

As a result of the abolition of the old Lloyd's SG form, it has been necessary to transplant into each of the new sets of clauses the Perils Clause, the Sue and Labor Clause, and the Waiver Clause; at the same time, it has been necessary to rephrase them in modern and unambiguous language. The old Sue and Labor Clause appears in an entirely new guise as the Duty of Assured Clause. On the other hand, the phrase "perils of the seas" remains ambiguous for those who are unfamiliar with the many English-law cases that define that term, even though for avoidance of one possible area of doubt, "the seas" have been described as rivers, lakes, or other navigable waters.

The new clauses were dated January 1, 1982, and were intended to be more intelligible to an insured person who enjoys only a casual acquaintance with English law relating to marine insurance.

Update in 2009

The Joint Cargo Committee released Revised Institute Cargo Clauses "A," "B," and "C," along with accompanying Institute Cargo Clauses—War and Institute Cargo Clauses—Strikes on November 24, 2008. The new clauses are dated January 1, 2009 after a wide consultation aiming to make the use of the clauses mor simple and clear to understand.

2. Institute Cargo Clauses, January 1, 1982

Following are the cargo clauses most widely applied for regarding marine insurance policies. The clauses were the joint work of cargo underwriters in the London marine insurance market as well as the representatives from Lloyd's.

They are graded in accordance with their scope of coverage, with "A" providing the widest coverage, followed by "B," and then the narrowest, "C" clauses.

1.1 Institute Cargo Clauses "A"
1.1.1 Risks Covered
1.1.1.1 *Clause 1—Risks Clause*

The expression "all risks" covers any loss or damage occasioned fortuitously but not that which occurs inevitably. In this respect, the coverage provided is less broad than an insurance that covers, for example, "all loss and damage, however caused."

"Loss of or damage to" covers all physical loss and damage to goods. It does not include financial loss unaccompanied by any physical loss or damage, such as loss of market, even though the cause of the financial loss was a peril insured against.

1.1.1.2 *Clause 2—General Average Clause*

Where there is a general average loss, the party onto whom it falls is entitled (subject to the conditions imposed by maritime law) to a ratable contribution from the other parties interested. This is called "general average contribution."

"Salvage charges" refers to the charges recoverable under maritime law by a salver independent of contract.

1.1.1.3   *Clause 3—Both to Blame Collision Clause*

This clause was inserted to cover the cargo owner from possible claims raised from a collision action whereby, in the United States, owners of cargo damaged by the collision may in principle proceed with their claim for damages against either the carrying vessel or the noncarrying vessel involved in the collision.

Under English law, the degree of blame is divided between the vessels in proportion to their degrees of fault, as decided by negotiation or an appropriate tribunal. Thus, if Vessel A is held to be 40 percent to blame, and Vessel B 60 percent, cargo owner on Vessel A could recover 60 percent of its damages from Vessel B. Usually, that cargo would not be able to recover the 40 percent balance from the carrying vessel because of the terms of the contract of affreightment, which contain exceptions regarding negligence in navigation.

Historically in the United States, if both vessels were to blame, the blame was always divided on a fifty-fifty basis, irrespective of the degree of fault. Additionally, Vessel A was allowed to recover 100 percent of its losses from Vessel B. Vessel B would then recover 50 percent of the Cargo A claim from Vessel A, so that Vessel A would end up paying 50 percent of the damage suffered by its own cargo.

The clause covers the contingency of the assured, having sustained a loss or damage by collision, seeking to recover for his or her own account from the noncarrying vessel, and being met by a valid Both to Blame Collision Clause in the contract of affreightment.

Example:

Vessels A and B are in a collision for which they are equally to blame, so their respective losses follow.

A is damaged to the following extent:

Repair	$8,000
Demurrage	$2,000
Total cost	$10,000

B is damaged to the following extent:

Repair	$5,000
Demurrage	$1,000
Total cost	$6,000

Settlement:

B is liable for 50 percent of A's damage and demurrage	= $5,000
A is liable for 50 percent of B's damage and demurrage	= $3,000
Then, B pays to A	= $2,000

1.1.2 Exclusions

1.1.2.1 *Clause 4—General Exclusions Clause*

4.1.   "Willful misconduct" of the insured is defined as a course of action undertaken either deliberately, with the insured knowing it to be wrongful so far as others are concerned, or recklessly, without caring whether it is wrongful or not. People exhibit willful misconduct when they know and appreciate that it is misconduct on their parts in doing something or failing to do something, yet they (a) intentionally do, fail, or omit to perform an act; (b) persist in the act, failure, or omission regardless of the consequences; or (c) act with reckless carelessness, not caring what the result of this carelessness may be.

4.2.   Ordinary leakage, ordinary loss in weight or volume, or ordinary wear and tear of the subject matter insured:

Ordinary loss in weight can arise from some cargoes shedding part of their water content while in transit. Bulk oils and fats may stick to tank pipelines so that the full, original quantity can never be delivered. In appropriate circumstances, policies may specify an excess of 0.5 percent, for example, to cover normal loss, but it is important that clear wording is employed.

4.3.   Insufficiency or unsuitability of packing and preparation of the subject matter insured:

Unsuitability of packing or preparation can take many forms. A recent example involved the use of damp timber by the company responsible for palletizing the goods after the inland transit, when it was ready to be placed in containers. As a result, severe condensation occurred during the voyage, which penetrated the bagged titanium dioxide. If the palletizing had been carried out by the insured, there would have been no claim, but since the palletizing was done by a third party during the insured transit, the insured party could recover damages.

4.4.   Inherent vice or nature of the subject matter insured:

The question of what constitutes inherent vice often causes difficulties in practice. An English court provided the following definition:

The phrase where it is used in section 55(2)(c) of MIA of 1906 refers to a peril by which a loss is proximately caused; it is not descriptive of the loss itself. It means the risk of deterioration of the goods shipped as a result of their natural behavior in the ordinary course of the contemplated voyage without the intervention of any fortuitous external accident or casualty. This is simply to say that the cause of loss or damage is from within the goods and not an outer source.

4.5. Proximately caused by delay:

The word "proximately" is used in this clause presumably in order to conform to section 55(2)(b) of the Marine Insurance Act of 1906.

This exclusion is applied in a case in which part of a cargo of fruit deteriorated, owing to a delay occasioned on the voyage because the ship needed repair on account of collision damage.

The only instance of "claim for expenses consequent upon delay for which the insurers will respond" arises when a ship has been detained in the circumstances envisaged in the York-Antwerp Rules or other similar provisions affecting the general average.

4.6. Insolvency or financial default of the owners, managers, charterers, or operators of the vessel:

A person is said to be insolvent when he or she is unable to pay all debts in full. Insolvency would appear to be wider even than "financial default" and would include situations in which many shipowners or operators still manage to continue trading.

It appears that the intention of the draftspersons was to exclude all types of claims for the recovery and forwarding of goods arising from the abandonment of a voyage by shipowners or operators who run out of funds while the voyage was still viable.

4.7. Use of any weapon of war employing atomic or nuclear fission and/or fusion or other like reactions, radioactive force, or matter:

"Use of any weapon of war" presumably includes the testing of such weapons as well as their usage in war situations. If a ship and cargo were contaminated by fallout from the test of a nuclear device intended to form the basis of a weapon, the exclusion would apply. On the other hand, if the contamination occurred as a result of a radioactive emission owing to an accident at a nuclear power station, underwriters insuring on "all risks" conditions would respond for the loss or damage so caused.

1.1.2.2 ***Clause 5—Unseaworthiness and Unfitness Exclusion Clause***
Being "privy" to something involves having actual, confirmed knowledge of it or being suspicious of the true situation and "turning a blind eye" to it and refraining from inquiry.

The proviso "unless the assured or their servants are privy to such unseaworthiness or unfitness" takes the place of a positive statement and in the event of loss, the insured's right of recovery would not be prejudiced by the fact that the loss may have been attributable to the wrongful act or misconduct of the shipowners or their servants committed without the assured's knowledge.

1.1.2.3 ***Clause 6—War Exclusion Clause***
"Piracy" has been excepted from the list of war exclusions within the ICC "A" conditions.

The definition of piracy is "forcible robbery at sea, whether committed by marauders from outside the ship or by mariners or passengers within it. The essential element is that they violently dispossess the master and afterward carry away the ship itself, or any of the goods, with a felonious intent" (see Institute War Clauses—Cargo).

1.1.2.4 ___Clause 7—Strikes Exclusion Clause___
These will be discussed with the Institute Strikes Clauses. However, it is worth noting that claims that arise from the activity of terrorists or persons acting from political motives have been transferred from Marine Risks coverage to Strike Risks coverage.

1.1.3   Duration
1.1.3.1   ___Clause 8—Transit Clause___
This clause is, in fact, the old "warehouse to warehouse" clause, as it used to be called in previous editions of the ICC. It defines the points at which the risk attaches and terminates, and it adds definitive words as to the circumstances in which it remains in force, notwithstanding certain events beyond the control of the insured.

Commencement of Transit

"From the time goods leave the warehouse": The term "leaving" involves the physical movement of the goods with the intention to proceed on the transit. The mere loading of goods into a truck that then remains on the premises is not sufficient.

Termination of the Transit

Three possibilities are envisaged by the clause, and the insured transit will terminate as soon as any one of them occurs, even though the insured may intend to continue the transit, notwithstanding such an occurrence. The events, any of which will terminate the risk, are as follows:

a) Delivery to the consignees' final warehouse or other place of storage at the destination named in the policy

b) Delivery to a place of storage, which the insured intends to use "other than in the ordinary course of transit or for allocation or distribution"

c) Expiry of sixty days after completion of discharge from the ocean vessel at the conclusion of the sea leg of the transit. This sixty-day period is a limit as well as an automatic cutoff

1.1.3.2 *Clause 9—Termination of Contract of Carriage*

This clause sets out one of the circumstances in which underwriters will require prompt notice to be given by the insured with a request for continuation of cover, in order to maintain the insurance subject to any additional premium that may be required.

The clause explores the circumstances that either the voyage is abandoned (with or without good cause) by the shipowner or other carrier, or that the venture is frustrated. For example, this occurred when ships were "locked in" the Suez Canal during its closure. However, the continuation of coverage granted by the clause is severely limited; it will end either when the goods are sold and delivered at the port or place where the transit has terminated, or upon the expiry of sixty days if the goods have not been sold within that time. It can also end if the goods are forwarded within sixty days or any agreed-upon extension of time, until delivery at either the original destination or a destination subsequently agreed to.

THE MARINE INSURANCE HANDBO_

1.1.3.3 *Clause 10—Change of Voyage*

What is a change of voyage? Section 45 of the Marine Insurance Act provides definitions:

1. Where, after the commencement of the risk, the destination of the ship is voluntarily changed from the destination contemplated by the policy, there is said to be a change of voyage.
2. Unless the policy otherwise provides, where there is a change of voyage, the insurer is discharged from liability as from the time of the change, that is to say, as from the time when the determination to change it is manifested, and it is immaterial that the ship may not in fact have left the course of the voyage contemplated by the policy when the loss occurs.

These circumstances require the insured to give notice to his or her underwriters, arguing that such a change of voyage by the shipowner or charterer was an event such as a deviation or even a termination of the contract of carriage, which is entirely beyond his or her control.

1.1.4   Claims

1.1.4.1 *Clause 11—Insurable Interest Clause*

This clause closely follows section 6 of the Marine Insurance Act, which states the following:

1. The assured must be interested in the subject matter insured at the time of the loss, though he or she need not be interested when the insurance is effected.
2. Where the assured has no interest at the time of the loss, he or she cannot acquire interest by any act or election after the assured is aware of the loss.

Clause 12—Forwarding Charges Clause

a) If, by the occurrence of an insured peril, the voyage is terminated short of destination, and the cost of recovering the goods, reconditioning them if necessary, and forwarding them to their destination would exceed their value on arrival, there is a constructive total loss.
b) If it is impossible to forward the goods to their destination, there is likewise constructive total loss of the goods, even though they are in sound condition.
c) If it is impossible to forward the goods to their destination at an expense less than their value on arrival, there can be no total loss, and any claim upon the policy can only be a partial loss.

1.1.4.3   Clause 13—Constructive Total Loss Clause

The subject matter insured must be "reasonably abandoned" by reason of the circumstances specified in order to found a claim for a Constrictive Total Loss (CTL).

"Abandoned" denotes the voluntary relinquishment by the assured to the insurer of whatever remains of the subject matter insured, together with all proprietary rights and remedies in respect thereof.

Section 62 of the Marine Insurance Act provides that "where the assured elects to abandon the subject matter insured to the insurer, he or she must give notice of abandonment. If the assured fails to do so, the loss can only be treated as a partial loss."

The circumstances giving rise to a claim for constructive total loss can fall under either of the following descriptions:

"On account of its actual total loss appearing to be unavoidable."

When such a commodity ceases to be merchantable as a thing of the kind originally insured, it is said to have lost its species, and in those circumstances, it has been held that there is an actual total loss of the goods.

or

"Because the cost of recovering, reconditioning, and forwarding the subject matter to the destination to which it is insured would exceed its value on arrival."

This is a purely objective test that would, strictly speaking, have to be proved by figures showing what the goods were worth at their destination.

"Value on arrival" also involves an estimation of what the goods would sell for in whatever condition they would be on arrival at their destination.

An additional circumstance (not mentioned in clause 13), which may also found a claim for a constructive total loss, is set out in section 60(2)(i) of the Marine Insurance Act: "Where the assured is deprived of the possession of his or her ship or goods by a peril insured against, and (a) it is unlikely that he or she can recover the ship or goods, or (b) the cost of recovering the ship or goods would exceed their value when recovered."

1.1.4.4   *Clause 14—Increased Value Clause*

The intention of this clause is to ensure that all claims are divided *pro rata* over original- and increased-value underwriters, and that all recoveries shall be dealt with likewise.

1.1.5 Benefit of Insurance

Clause 15—Not to Inure Clause

The object of the clause is to prevent a carrier or other bailee contracting out of his or her liability by inserting a clause in the contract of affreightment, or other agreement, claiming the benefit of insurance.

1.1.6 Minimizing Losses

Clause 16—Duty of Assured

The clause places a duty upon the assured to preserve and exercise the rights that underwriters have, or will become entitled to, by subrogation. Expenses reasonably incurred by the assured in pursuance of this duty will be met by the underwriters.

"The duty of the assured and his or her servants and agents": This expression is wider than it appears at first sight. Under English law, the master of a ship is invested with a wide range of duties and responsibilities to take care of the goods entrusted to his or her charge. These duties derive in part under the law of bailment, since a shipowner who receives the goods for carriage is a bailee for rewards, and the master of the ship is the person responsible for exercising the duties of care that follow from that legal relationship.

In the event of a serious casualty, a shipowner may be responsible for the payment of substantial sums for the preservation and care of cargo, all of which (in absence of his or her actionable fault) he or she will be entitled to recover as a special charge on cargo.

"For the purpose of averting or minimizing such loss": This expression refers to a loss or damage to which the underwriters would respond under the policy, thus reproducing the effect of section 78(3) of the Marine Insurance Act, which states:

"Expenses incurred for the purpose of averting or minimizing any loss not covered by the policy are not recoverable under the Suing and Laboring Clause" and "Rights against carriers, bailees, and other third parties":

On payment of a loss, underwriters are (by section 79 of the Marine Insurance Act) subrogated to all rights and remedies of the assured in respect to the loss so paid for. However, owing to the lapse of time that may occur between the occurrence of the loss and the claim being paid, it is essential that rights and remedies against third parties should be preserved. Expenses reasonably incurred by the assured in pursuance of this duty will be met by the underwriters.

1.1.6.1   *Clause 17—Waiver Clause*
Any steps taken by the assured "in protecting, or recovering, the subject matter insured" shall not constitute a waiver or withdrawal of the notice of abandonment that he or she has given; similarly, the underwriters are free to take such steps without their being regarded as an acceptance of the abandonment that had previously declined.

1.1.7   Avoidance of Delay
Clause 18—Reasonable Dispatch
It is a condition of this insurance that the assured shall act with reasonable dispatch in all circumstances within his or her control.

1.1.8   Law and Practice
Clause 19—English Law and Practice Clause
This clause is common to all the new institute clauses issued from January 1, 1982, onward, except those intended to be attached to American forms.

The clause is a useful step toward avoiding disputes on this aspect of the contract and to ensure that existing case law and the MIA of 1906 will be fully applied, even if some other jurisdiction is involved.

That is the end of the numbered clauses. There then appears the following entry:

NOTE: It is necessary for the assured, when he or she becomes aware of an event that is "held covered" under this insurance, to give prompt notice to the underwriters, and the right to such coverage is dependent upon compliance with this obligation.

This note appears at the foot of all institute clauses covering goods. It is not only sound advice; it also states the existing law, since it is an implied term of any contract of marine insurance that the assured will be unable to invoke a "held covered" provision unless, within a reasonable time after knowledge of the event, he or she has given notice to the underwriters.

1.2   Institute Cargo Clauses "B" and "C"
1.2.1   Risk Covered
Loss of or damage to the subject matter insured reasonably <u>attributable</u> to the following.

1.2.1.1   *Fire*
The expression "fire" includes damage by heat through proximity to something that is on fire, but it does not include deterioration due to the chemical changes involved in the heating up of some commodity by natural causes nor spontaneous combustion; both were excluded by clause 4.4 as being caused by inherent vice or the nature of the subject matter insured. Loss or damage reasonably attributable to fire also comprises damage caused by the act of extinguishing fire or action reasonably taken to avoid the spread of

THE MARINE INSURANCE HANDBOOK

fire, and in acts taken in anticipation of, and to prevent, the outbreak of fire.

1.2.1.2   *Explosion*

"Explosion" denotes "an event that is violent, noisy, and caused by a very rapid chemical reaction or the bursting out of gas or vapor under pressure."

1.2.1.3   *Vessel or Craft Being Stranded, Grounded, Sunk, or Capsized*

"Stranded or grounded" read together comprise any fortuitous taking of the ground by the carrying vessel or craft, for however short a period of time. It is also submitted that an intentional taking of the ground, for example in a mud berth where it is customary for ships to lie aground at low tide, will be covered, if as a consequence the insured goods sustain damage.

The word "capsized" will mean that such a loss, when goods fall into the sea as a result of the carrying ship taking a totally unexplained list while in port, will be settled by the underwriters.

1.2.1.4   *Overturning or Derailment of Land Conveyance*

If in consequence of a derailment, the goods in the railway wagon have to be hurriedly unloaded and dumped by the side of the railway track in order to enable the wagon to be lifted back onto the rails, loss or damage caused by this operation should be responded to by the underwriters, as well as the damage caused by the direct shock of the derailment.

1.2.1.5   *Collision or Contact of Vessel, Craft, or Conveyance with Any External Object other than Water*

The contact must be with something external to the carrying vessel, craft, or conveyance. Collision and contact by vehicles on the land are included.

17

"Conveyance" in this section denotes any type of vehicle customarily used during the insured transit.

1.2.1.6   ***Discharge of Cargo at Port of Distress***
This is usually admissible in general average, and when this is the case, any damage or loss to cargo used in the process of discharging is likewise admitted. However, if the discharge of cargo at the port of refuge was for the purpose of examining the goods themselves for suspected damage or after the shipowner had validly abandoned the voyage, it is reasonable in these circumstances that the assured should be similarly covered.

1.2.1.7   ***Earthquake, Volcanic Eruption, and Lightning***
These risks are additions to the coverage that appears in the "B" clauses but not in "C" clauses.

Loss or damage to the subject matter insured <u>caused by</u>

1.2.1.8   ***General Average Sacrifice***
Any insurance subject to English law and practice will pay for general average in accordance with section 66(4) of the MIA of 1906.

1.2.1.9   ***Jettison or Washing Overboard (as in "B" Clauses)***
1.2.1.10   ***Jettison (as in "C" Clauses)***
"Jettison" is defined as the lawful throwing overboard of goods, whether in circumstances that make it general average or not. This could extend, for example, to the deliberate dumping over the side of packages condemned as hazardous by a local authority unless the assured was guilty of shipping them.

THE MARINE INSURANCE HANDBOOK

1.2.1.11   <u>*Entry of Sea, Lake, or River Water into Vessel Craft, Hold,*</u>
<u>*Conveyance, Lift Van, or Place of Storage*</u>
This appears in "B" clauses to extend the ocean transit to rivers and lakes. Suppose that, during the overland leg of the transit, a truck driver loses his or her way and drives the truck containing the insured goods into the middle of the river; underwriters will be liable for the damage to the goods due to their immersion.

1.2.1.12   <u>*Total Loss of Any Package Lost Overboard while Loading onto, or*</u>
<u>*Unloading from, Vessel or Craft*</u>
This appears in "B" clauses only.

1.2.2   General Average Clause

General average contribution that is payable by the insured cargo would only be recoverable if the general average act were undertaken to avoid one of the limited named perils.

1.2.3   "Both to Blame Collision" Clause

This is the same as it appears in clause "A."

1.2.4   General Exclusions Clause

"B" and "C" clauses add the following to the list of exclusion:

"Deliberate damage to or deliberate destruction of the subject matter insured or any part thereof by the wrongful act of any person or persons." This exclusion would include the following acts:

     a)   Barratry of the master and crew
     b)   Arson or sabotage, causing the ship to sink

c) Scuttling of the carrying ship or craft by its owner in fraud of his or her insurers

d) A jettison of the goods without reasonable cause

Note: This coverage can be reinstated and extended, on payment of an additional premium, by attachment of a separate clause to the policy. This is the *Institute Malicious Damage Clause.*

1.2.5 War Exclusion Clause

This wording is similar to the "A" clause but with one important additional exclusion, which is the risk of piracy.

CHAPTER 2

WAR AND SRCC

2.1 Institute War Clauses—Cargo
2.1.1 Risk Covered
2.1.1.1 *War*

This involves the employment of force between states or entities having at least *de facto* the characteristic of a state. The term may be narrower than "hostilities," which connotes the idea of enemy nations at war with one another.

2.1.1.2 *Civil war*

This term denotes the state of hostility between different sections or groups in the same state, each exercising at least quasi-government authority.

2.1.1.3 *Revolution, rebellion, and insurrection*

These words suggest a rising scale in the development of civil disorder. "Insurrection" is defined as a violent uprising by a group or movement acting for the specific purpose of overthrowing the constituted government and seizing its power.

"Rebellion" denotes a state of organized, armed, and open resistance against the authority and government or sovereign of the country to which one has allegiance; it is distinguished from civil war, usually by the small number of rebels.

"Revolution" is the complete subversion of established political authority and the establishment of a new government of existing political conditions.

2.1.1.4 *Civil strife arising therefrom*

These words cover civil strife or unrest that arises in consequence of any of the preceding risks. They have to be contrasted with "riot or civil commotions," for which coverage is provided in the institute strikes clauses (cargo). In practice, the dividing line may be hard to find between civil strife arising from an insurrection and a civil commotion that does not.

2.1.1.5 *By or against a belligerent power "Any Hostile Act"*

To bring a claim by using these terms, it would have to be shown:

  a) that the loss or damage had been proximately caused by an act (that is to say, some action on the part of somebody);

  b) that it was hostile (this may or may not involve a question of intent); and

  c) that it was directed either by or against a "power" that is "belligerent."

2.1.1.6 *Power*

This term includes a state (and probably also an entity) exercising quasi-governmental authority.

2.1.1.7 *Belligerent*
This term has two possible meanings, one restricted and one much with a much wider reach. The restricted definition is one who is "carrying on war according to the law of nations."

The term may also apply to anyone engaged in armed conflict.

2.1.1.8 *Capture and seizure*
"Capture" includes every act of seizing or taking by any enemy or belligerent entity.

"Seizure" is a broader term than "capture"; it denotes the attempt at every act of taking forcible possession, either by a lawful or by overpowering force.

2.1.1.9 *Arrest, restraint, or detainment*
These terms refer to political or executive acts, and do not include losses caused by riot or by ordinary judicial processes.

2.1.1.10 *Derelict mines, torpedoes, bombs, or other weapons of war*
The word "derelict" has presumably been added in order to reverse the effect of a court decision in which it was held that the damage sustained by a dredger that sucked up ammunition that had been dumped after the end of World War II was not the consequence of a warlike operation.

2.1.1.11 *Frustration*
The true meaning of the "frustration clause" is that it operates when, and only when, the claim is based entirely on the loss of the insured voyage by frustration of the venture.

2.1.1.12 *Loss, damage, or expense arising from any hostile use of any weapon of war employing atomic or nuclear fission and/or fusion or other like reaction or radioactive force or matter*

The inclusion of the term "hostile use" would seem to suggest that a loss by a "nonhostile" use of such a weapon, such as by its explosion while being deployed by friendly forces, would result in a claim for which underwriters under the IWC—Cargo would respond.

2.1.2 Transit Clause

The risk does not attach until the goods are loaded onto the overseas vessel and does not extend beyond fifteen days after arrival of the vessel at its final port or place of discharge. If there is a discharge of goods at an intermediate port or place (even a port or place of refuge), the assured can obtain continuation of the cover on payment of an additional premium if required.

2.2 Institute Strikes Clauses—Cargo
2.2.1 Risks Clause

2.2.1.1 *Strikers, locked-out workmen, or persons taking part in labor disturbances*

These words have to be construed in the ordinary, everyday sense in which they are understood.

2.2.1.2 *Riot*

In order to constitute a riot, five elements are necessary:

    a) A number of persons not less than five
    b) A common purpose
    c) Execution or inception of the common purpose

d) An intent on the part of the number of persons to help one another, by force if necessary, against any person who may oppose them in the execution of the common purpose
e) Force or violence

2.2.1.3 *Civil commotion*

Civil commotion need not involve a revolt against the government, but there must be a disturbance with sufficient cohesion to prevent it from being the work of a mindless mob.

2.2.1.4 *Any terrorist or any person acting from a political motive*

A "terrorist" could be recognized from his or her actions, particularly in today's climate of "terrorist" activities.

2.2.1.5 *Any person acting from a political motive*

This covers the phenomenon of the "gentle terrorist," who does not wish to do anyone harm, but wishes merely to demonstrate his or her objection to somebody or some cause by doing physical damage to property.

2.2.2 General Exclusions

General exclusions include loss, damage, or expense from the absence, shortage, or withholding of labor of any description whatsoever resulting from any strife, lockout, labor disturbances, riot, or civil commotion.

While the insurance pays for loss or damage caused by violent behavior of strikers, the underwriters will not respond to any claim that arises from the withdrawal of the strikers' labor.

2.2.3   **Unseaworthiness and Unfitness Exclusion Clause**

2.2.4   **Duration**

2.2.5   **Claims—Insurable Interest Clause**

2.2.6   **Increased Value Clause**

2.2.7   **Not to Inure Clause**

2.2.8   **Duty of Assured Clause**

2.2.9   **Waiver Clause**

2.2.10   **Reasonable Dispatch Clause**

2.2.11   **English Law and Practice**
These clauses are the same as in the "A" institute cargo clauses.

CHAPTER 3

INSTITUTE CARGO CLAUSES 2009

3.1 A Comparison of the 1982 and 2009 Clauses
Institute Cargo Clauses "A"

The new clauses of 2009 updated some terms for the general use throughout the clauses language.

I. The term "goods" was replaced by the "subject matter insured". The term is considered to be wider than "goods". For example: Cash money were not referred to as "goods" in case of insurance during transit.
II. "Insurers" is used to replace the old description of "underwriters".
III. The 1982 clauses used marginal side headings but this is replaced by subheadlines.

Clause 1: Risks Covered
1982

1. This insurance covers all risks of loss or damage to the subject matter insured *except as provided* in clauses 4, 5, 6, and 7 below.

2009

1. This insurance covers all risks of loss or damage to the subject matter insured *except as excluded* in clauses 4, 5, 6, and 7 below.

"Except as provided" is replaced by "except as excluded," which gives a clearer indication that the clauses referred to are exclusions.

Clause 2: General Average Clause
1982

2. This insurance covers general average and salvage charges, adjusted or determined according to the contract of affreightment and/or the governing law and practice, incurred to avoid or in the connection of avoidance of loss from any cause, except those excluded in clauses 4, 5, 6, and 7 or elsewhere in this insurance.

2009

2. This insurance covers general average and salvage charges, adjusted or determined according to the contract of affreightment and/or the governing law and practice, incurred to avoid or in connection with the avoidance of loss from any cause, except those excluded in clauses 4, 5, 6 and 7 below. (The concluding words of the 1982 "or elsewhere in this insurance" are omitted.)

Clause 3: Both to Blame Collision
1982

3. This insurance is extended to indemnify the assured against such proportion of liability under the contract

of affreightment "Both to Blame Collision" clause as is in respect to a loss recoverable hereunder. In the event of any claim by shipowners under the said clause, the assured agrees to notify the underwriters, who shall have the right, at their own cost and expense, to defend the assured against such claim.

2009

3. This insurance indemnifies the assured, in regard to any risk insured herein, against liability incurred under any "both to blame" collision clause in the contract of carriage. In the event of any claim by carriers under the said clause, the assured agree to notify the insurers, who shall have the right, at their own cost and expense, to defend the assured against such claim.

The 2009 wording has been adapted slightly in the interest of clarity.

Clause 4: Exclusions

1982 and 2009:

4. In no case shall this insurance cover...

4.1 Loss, damage, or expense attributable to willful misconduct of the assured...

Here, there is no change; the wording reproduces part of the MIA of 1906.

1982 and 2009:

4.2 Ordinary leakage, ordinary loss in weight or volume, or ordinary wear and tear of the subject matter insured...

Here, there is no change wordings remained same.

1982

4.3 Loss, damage, or expense caused by insufficiency or unsuitability of packing or preparation of the subject matter insured (for the purpose of this clause, 4.3, "packing" shall be deemed to include stowage in a container or lift van but only when such stowage is carried out prior to attachment of this insurance or by the assured or their servants).

2009

4.3 Loss, damage, or expense caused by insufficiency or unsuitability of packing or preparation of the subject matter insured to withstand the ordinary incidents of the insured transit where such packing or preparation is carried out by the assured or their employees or prior to the attachment of this insurance (for the purpose of these clauses, "packing" shall be deemed to include stowage in a container, and "employees" shall not include independent contractors).

The term "lift van" no longer appears, and the archaic term "servants" is replaced by the word "employees," with additional clarification that independent contractors are not to be considered as employees.

The new clause sets out the standard by which any insufficiency or unsuitability is to be judged—the packing or preparation must be sufficient "to withstand the ordinary incidents of the insured transit."

This important exclusion will apply when:

- The packing or preparation is carried out by the assured or his or her employees; or

- The packing or preparation is carried out prior to attachment of the risk.

1982 and 2009

4.4 Loss, damage, or expense caused by inherent vice of the subject matter insured.

Wording in both versions remained same without change consistent with the articles of the Marine Insurance Act of 1906.

1982

4.5 Loss, damage, or expense *proximately* caused by delay, even though the delay be caused by a risk insured against (except expenses payable under clause 2 above).

2009

4.5 Loss, damage, or expense caused by delay, even though the delay be caused by a risk insured against (except expenses payable under clause 2 above).

The exclusion regarding delay remains unchanged, except for the removal of the word "proximately."

1982

4.6 Loss, damage, or expense arising from insolvency or financial default of the owners, managers, charterers, or operators of the vessel.

2009

4.6 Loss, damage, or expense caused by insolvency or financial default of the owners, managers, charterers, or operators of the vessel where, at the time of loading of the subject matter insured onboard the vessel, the assured are aware, or in the ordinary course of business should be aware, that such insolvency or financial default could prevent the normal prosecution of the voyage.

This exclusion shall not apply where the contract of insurance has been assigned to the party claiming hereunder who has bought or agreed to buy the subject matter in good faith under a binding contract.

The innocent assured or assignee is still protected by the policy in the event of financial default or insolvency, bringing the voyage to an end.

Thus, a claim will only fail if, at the time of loading, the assured was aware or should have been aware that the voyage might be halted by the financial circumstances of the carrier.

1982

4.7 Loss, damage, or expense *arising from* the use of *any weapon of war* employing atomic or nuclear fission and/or other reaction or radioactive force.

2009

4.7 Loss, damage, or expense *directly or indirectly caused by or arising from* the use of *any weapon or device* employing atomic or nuclear fission and/or fusion or other like reaction or radioactive force or matter.

The 2009 exclusion addresses some of the concerns that appeared in the Institute Radioactive Contamination, Chemical, Biological, Biochemical, and Electromagnetic Weapons Clause of October 11, 2003.

THE MARINE INSURANCE HANDBOOK

- "Arising from" becomes "directly or indirectly caused by or arising from."
- "Weapon of war" becomes the broader phrase "any weapon or device," which would include the so-called "dirty bomb" that might be used by terrorists to cause widespread contamination.
- The effect of the change is to widen the exclusion.

Clause 5: Unseaworthiness and Unfitness Exclusion Clause

1982

5.1   In no case shall this insurance cover loss, damage, or expense arising from unseaworthiness of vessel or craft, unfitness of vessel, craft, conveyance, container, or lift van for the safe carriage of the subject matter insured, where the assured or their servants are privy to such unseaworthiness or unfitness at the time the subject matter insured is loaded therein.

5.2   The underwriters waive any breach of the implied warranties of seaworthiness of the ship and fitness of the ship to carry the subject matter insured to the destination, unless the assured or their servants are privy to such unseaworthiness or unfitness.

2009

5.1   In no case shall this insurance cover loss, damage, or expense arising from:

5.1.1   Unseaworthiness of vessel or craft, or unfitness of vessel or craft for the safe carriage of the subject matter insured, where the assured are privy to such unseaworthiness or unfitness at the time the subject matter insured is loaded therein.

33

5.1.2 Unfitness of container or conveyance for the safe carriage of the subject matter insured, where loading therein or thereon is carried out prior to attachment of this insurance or by the assured or their employees, and they are privy to such unfitness at the time of loading.

5.2 Exclusion 5.1.1 above shall not apply where the contract of insurance has been assigned to the party hereunder who has bought or agreed to buy the subject matter insured in good faith under a binding contract.

5.3 The insurers waive any breach of the implied warranties of seaworthiness of the ship and fitness of the ship to carry the subject matter insured to destination.

The new clauses remove the word " lift-van" matching with the clauses that were quoted above. The term "servants" was replaced by "employees".

The insurance cover will not operate when:

- The assured was aware of the condition of the vessel or craft to be unfit or unseaworthy at time of loading.
- The container or conveyance is not safe for the transit risks, and

  a) the loading of the goods is carried out prior to attachment of risk; or
  b) the loading is carried out by the assured or his or her employees who were privy to such condition of unfitness.

However, clause 5.2 protects the innocent party whom the policy had been assigned to his/her order assigned as part of a binding sale contract. It is assumed that the person is unlikely to be in a position to control or verify the suitability of the vessel or container when the seller selects such conveyance.

The effect of the clause is to narrow the scope of the exclusion for the benefit of the innocent assured..

Clause 6: War Exclusion Clause
1982 and 2009

6. wordings remained same in both versions to match with the fact that war risks can be covered by the Institute War Clauses (Cargo) which remained with same effect.

Clause 7: Strikes Exclusion
1982

7. In no case shall this insurance cover loss, damage, or expense...

7.1 Caused by strikers, locked-out workmen, or persons taking part in labor disturbances, riots, or civil commotions...

7.2 Resulting from strikes, lockout labor disturbances, riots, or civil commotions...

7.3 Caused by any terrorist or any person acting from a political motive...

2009

7. In no case shall this insurance cover loss, damage, or expense...

7.1 Caused by strikers, locked-out workmen, or persons taking part in labor disturbances, riots, or civil commotions...

7.2 Resulting from strikes, lockout, labor disturbances, riots, or civil ommotions

7.3 Caused by any act of terrorism being an act of any person acting on behalf of, or in connection with, any organization that carries out activities directed toward the overthrowing or influencing, by force or violence, of any government, whether or not legally constituted.

7.4 Caused by any person acting from a political, ideological, or religious motive.

The terrorism exclusion has been extended to reflect the worldwide climate of such risk. The wide range of threat could now be encountered with the motives behind any attack.

Institute Strikes Clauses (Cargo) of January 1, 2009, have been amended to cover the required risks . It is necessary to note that the cover is in respect of physical loss , damage or expenses to avoid the loss or damage but not for losses that incur beause of shipment is delayed by strikes action or terrorist attack.

Clause 8: Duration

1982

8.   Transit Clause

8.1 This insurance attaches from the time the *goods leave* the warehouse or place of storage at the place named herein for the commencement of the transit, continues during the ordinary course of transit, and terminates either:

8.1.1 *On delivery* to the consignee or other final warehouse or place of storage at the destination named herein;

8.1.2 *On delivery* to any other warehouse or place of storage, whether prior to or at the destination named herein, which the assured elect to use, either

8.1.2.1 For storage other than in the ordinary course of transit; or

8.1.2.2 For allocation or distribution; or

8.1.3 On the expiry of sixty days after completion of discharge overside of the goods hereby insured from the oversea vessel at the final port of discharge, whichever shall first occur.

2009

8. Transit Clause

8.1 Subject to clause 11 below, this insurance attaches from the time the *subject matter insured moved* in the warehouse or at the place of storage (at the place named in the contract of insurance) for the purpose of the immediate loading into or onto the carrying vehicle or other conveyance for the commencement of transit, continues during the ordinary course of transit, and terminates either:

8.1.1 *On completion of unloading* from the carrying vehicle or other conveyance in or at the final warehouse or place of storage at the destination named in the contract of insurance;

8.1.2 *on completion of unloading* from the carrying vehicle or other conveyance in or at any other warehouse or place of storage, whether prior to or at the destination named in the contract of insurance, which the assured or their employees elect to use either for storage other than in the ordinary course of transit or for allocation or distribution; or

8.1.3 when the assured or the assured's employees elect to use any carrying vehicle or other conveyance for storage other than in the ordinary course of transit; or

8.1.4 on the expiry of sixty days after completion of discharge overside of the subject matter insured from the oversea vessel at the final port of discharge, whichever shall first occur.

The new clauses extended the cover to include the risk of loss or damage during the process of loading and unloading. However, cover does not extend to temporary storage prior to transit on vehicles or to storage in holding areas within a warehouse .

The sub-clauses 8.1.1 and 8.1.2 replaced the term"on delivery" to become on "completion of unloading."

The new wordings that appear in the sub clause 8.1.3 are to clarify that insurance also terminates if goods remain in the carrying vehicle and the assured or their employees elect to use it for storage . It should be noted that the new clause refer to the assured or their employees or management who are making decision on storage or distribution whereas the 1982 version refer only to the assured.

The new version of 2009 is intended to introduce special wording to modify the terms relating to policy attachment or termination. Also, care needs to be taken to ensure that the wording is clear and meets the requirements of the parties. Consideration must be given to the terms of the sale contract and the obligations of both parties , seller and buyer subject to the agreed Incoterms.

1982

8.2 If, after discharge overside from the oversea vessel at the final port of discharge, but prior to termination of this insurance, the goods are to be forwarded to a destination other than that to which they are insured hereunder, this insurance, while remaining subject to termination as provided for above, shall not extend beyond the commencement of transit to such other destination.

2009

8.2 If, after discharge overside from the oversea vessel the final port of discharge, but prior to termination of this insurance, the subject matter insured is to be forwarded to a destination other than that to which it is insured, this insurance, while remaining subject to termination as provided in clauses 8.1.1 to 8.1.4, shall not extend beyond the time the subject matter insured is first moved for the purpose of the commencement of transit to such other destination.

The language has only some reformation changes, but the effect is same.

1982

8.3 This insurance shall remain in force (subject to termination as provided for above and to the provision of clause 9 below) during delay beyond the control of the assured, any deviation, forced discharge, reshipment, or transshipment, and during any variation of the venture arising from the exercise of a liberty granted to shipowners or charterers under the contract of affreightment.

2009

8.3 This insurance shall remain in force (subject to termination as provided for in clauses 8.1.1 to 8.1.4 above and to the provision of clause 9 below) during delay beyond the control of the assured, any deviation, forced discharge, reshipment, or transshipment and during any variation of the adventure arising from the exercise of a liberty granted to carrier under the contract of carriage.

Some minor changes in the terminology by replacing "contract of affreightment to become "contract of carriage" but the effect remains the same.

Clause 9: Termination of Contract of Carriage

1982 and 2009

9. Termination of Contract of Carriage

- The term "Delivery" in clause 9 becomes "unloading" to be consistent with clause 8, and
- The term "named herein" in clause 9.2 becomes "named in the contract of insurance."

It is necessary and prudent to give immediate notice to the insurers in the event of a serious casualty or potentially significant delay.

Such action will assist insurers in deciding the steps to be aken in accordance with the situation either to monitor the case or to appoint a surveyor to attend and report on the particular requirement in respect of condition of goods and cause of damage.

Clause 10: Change of Voyage Clause

1982

10. Change of Voyage Clause

Where, after attachment of this insurance, the destination is changed by the assured, held covered at a premium, and on conditions to be arranged, subject to prompt notice being given to the underwriters.

2009

Change of Voyage

10.1 Where, after attachment of this insurance, the destination is changed by the assured, this must be notified promptly to insurers for rates and terms to be agreed. Should a loss occur prior to such agreement being obtained, coverage may be provided, but only if coverage would have been available at a reasonable commercial market rate on reasonable market terms.

10.2 Where the subject matter insured commences the transit contemplated by this insurance (in accordance with clause 8.1), but, without the knowledge of the assured or the assured's employees, the ship sails for another destination, this insurance will nevertheless be deemed to have attached at commencement of such transit.

The new wordings in the clause 10.1 avoids the use of the term "held covered," which has often various interpretations. The new wordings and give a clear indication of the necessary action the assured has to take and the coverage implication.

The clause 10.2 deals with the so-called "phantom ship" situation, in which a vessel (often with false papers) carries

Clause 11: Claims

1982 and 2009

11. Insurable Interest Clause

The same wording in both versions without change.

Clause 12: Forwarding Charges Clause

1982 and 2009

12. Forwarding Charges Clause

There were only minor changes without effect on cover. The term "underwriters" was changed to "insurers," "hereunder" has been deleted, and "employees" replaced "servants".

Clause 13: Constructive Total Loss

1982 and 2009

13. Constructive Total Loss

The wordings in bth versions were same withut change.

Clause 14: Increased Value

1982 and 2009

14. Increased Value

The only change in the term "herein" which became "under this insurance."

Clause 15: Benefit of Insurance

1982

15. Benefit of Insurance

This insurance shall not inure to the benefit of the carrier or other bailee.

2009

15. Benefit of Insurance

15.1 This insurance covers the assured, which includes the person claiming indemnity, either as the person by or on whose behalf the contract of insurance was affected or as an assignee.

15.2 Shall not extend to or otherwise benefit the carrier or other bailee.

The new version of 2009 inserted the definition of assured for more clarity. The term "inure" is changed to plain English wording.

Clause 16: Minimizing Losses

1982 and 2009

Minimizing Losses

16. Duty of Assured Clause

The wordings of this clause has no change in both versions to correspond with section 78 of the Marine Insurance Act of 1906. The clause included the requirement to ensure that rights to claim against carriers and other third parties are reserved.

Clause 17: Waiver Clause

1982 and 2009

17. Waiver Clause

The word "insurer" is replaced with "underwriters" with no other changes.

Clause 18: Avoidance of Delay

1982 and 2009

Avoidance of Delay

18. Reasonable Dispatch Clause

The wordings in both versions were the same.

Clause 19: Law and Practice

1982 and 2009

Law and Practice

19. English Law and Practice Clause

The wordings remained same without changes.

THE MARINE INSURANCE HANDBOOK

Note:

1982

It is necessary for the assured, when he or she becomes aware of an event that is "held covered" under this insurance, to give prompt notice to the underwriters, and the right to such coverage is dependent upon compliance with this obligation.

2009

Where a continuation of cover is requested under clause 9, or a change of destination is notified under clause 10, there is an obligation to give prompt notice to the insurers, and the right to such coverage is dependent upon compliance with this obligation.

The minor revisions intended to reflect the updates of the relative clauses which avoided the use of "held covered'. However, there is no change in the extent or breadth of the cover.

CHAPTER 4

INSTITUTE CLAUSES FOR PARTICULAR COMMODITIES

These clauses have been agreed upon by the trade associations concerned. In the commentary, only those clauses are mentioned that differ from the standard Institute Cargo Clauses.

4.1 Institute Frozen food Clauses "A"
(Excluding frozen meat)

Clause 1—Risks Clauses

This insurance covers, except as provided in 4, 5, 6, and 7 below, the following:

1.1. "All risks" of loss or damage to the subject matter insured, other than loss or damage resulting from any variation in temperature, however caused.

1.2. Loss of, or damage to, the subject matter insured resulting from any variation in temperature attributable to the following:

1.3. Breakdown of refrigerating machinery resulting in its stoppage for a period of not less than twenty-four consecutive hours;

1.4. Fire or explosion;

1.5. Vessel or craft being stranded, grounded, sunk, or capsized;

1.6. Overturning or derailment of land conveyance;

1.7. Collision or contact of vessel, craft, or conveyance with any external object other than water; or

1.8. Discharge of cargo at port of distress.

The risks clause is not quite as broad as "all risks," since claims for loss or damage resulting from variations in temperature are limited to those attributable to the causes named above.

The most important included peril causing variations in temperature is as follows:

"Breakdown of refrigerating machinery resulting in its stoppage for a period of not less than twenty-four consecutive hours."

The term "breakdown of machinery" by itself does not necessarily imply that the machinery comes to a full stop. The addition of the words "resulting in its stoppage" has the effect of excluding claims arising from variations in temperature due to the mere malfunction of the refrigerating machinery. It is also to be noted that the assured has to provide evidence from a carrier or other independent surveyor that the stoppage of the refrigerating machinery extended for a continuous period of not less than twenty-four hours.

Clause 2—General Average Clause

Clause 3—Both to Blame Collision

These clauses are the same as in the Institute Cargo Clauses

Clause 4—General Exclusion Clause

The main noted differences are:

Exclusion 4.4—The "Inherent Vice" exclusion adds "except loss, damage, or expense resulting from variations in temperature specifically covered under Clause 1.2 (above).

Thus, it is clear that underwriters will not raise this defense against any claim resulting from variations in temperature that have come about through one of the specific causes mentioned in clause 1.2.

Then follow two more exclusions that are particular to the commodity:

Exclusion 4.8 exempts the underwriters from liability for any claim arising from the failure of the assured or the assured's servants to take reasonable precautions to ensure that the goods are kept in properly refrigerated or cool and insulated spaces.

Exclusion 4.9 provides that no claim under the policy will be recoverable if the assured failed to address a prompt notice to the underwriters within thirty days after the termination of the insurance. This recognizes that a prudent cargo receiver should ascertain the proper condition of the goods as soon as possible after they arrive into his or her cold storage.

Clause 5—Unseaworthiness and Unfitness Exclusion Clause

Clause 6—War Exclusion Clause

Clause 7—Strikes Exclusion Clause

These are the same as the corresponding clauses in the Institute Cargo Clauses.

Clause 8—Transit Clause

This clause differs from the corresponding clause in the ICC.

The insured transit commences at the time the goods are loaded into the conveyance, whatever it may be, for the first leg of the journey.

The words "warehouse or place of storage" are replaced in the Institute Frozen Food Clauses by "freezing works or cold stores" to describe the location at which the goods are loaded, and by "cold store or place of storage" at destination.

The transit cutoff is a mere five days after discharge of the goods from the ocean steamer, instead of the period of sixty days, as provided in the ICC.

Clause 9—Termination of Carriage Clause

This clause is in the same form as the corresponding clause in the ICC, except that in the event of the termination of the contract of carriage in the circumstances set out in the clause, and subject to prompt notice being given to the underwriters requesting a continuation of coverage, the period of time for which such extension may be granted is thirty days instead of sixty days, as provided in the ICC.

Clauses 10 to 19

Clauses 10 to 19 are the same as in the ICC "A," with an additional special note added to clarify that, if the goods have sustained no loss or damage by insured perils, the fact that they may be rejected from importation by government regulation (for example, for not attaining some standard prescribed by a sanitary authority) or may be subject to an embargo, will not give the assured a right to claim under the policy.

That is, there is *no rejection* coverage under this clause.

4.2   Institute Bulk Oil Clauses

These are new additions to the institute portfolios. Previously, the only clauses for oil cargo were forms of Bulk Oil Clauses (SP-13C of January 1962), which had their origins in the United States.

It may be argued that the coverage provided by the institute's clauses are more broad or at least have more clarity of expression.

Clause 1—Risks Clause

The list of perils insured is generally in line with the provision of the ICC "B." However, the following variations may be noted:

a) Where the ICC refers to damage, the Bulk Oil clauses substitute "contamination."

b) There is no reference to "conveyance," other than by vessel or craft.

c) In place of "entry of seawater, etc." in the ICC, the Bulk Oil Clauses cover "contamination…from stress of weather." This can include, for example, claims for depreciation in value of an oil cargo of a specific quality, which becomes contaminated with the residues that normally lie inert at the bottom of the ships' tanks, through movement of the ship in severe weather.

d) Two additional perils are specifically included:

- Leakage from connecting pipelines in loading shipment or discharge. The words used express two limitations upon the risk of "leakage": (i) the leakage must occur in the course of loading shipment or discharge of the cargo; and (ii) the leakage must be from "connecting pipelines."
- Negligence of master officers or crew in pumping cargo ballast or fuel. In order to found a claim under this subclause, the loss or contamination has to be caused by the negligence of those concerned in "pumping."

Clause 2—General Average Clause

Clause 3—Both to Blame Collision Clause

These are in the same terms as the clauses in the ICC.

Clause 4—General Exclusion Clause

The list of exclusions corresponds to those that are set out in the ICC "B." However, the following may be noted:

a) There is no exclusion with respect to insufficiency of packing, since this would clearly be irrelevant; and
b) the exclusion of "deliberate destruction of the subject matter insured…by the wrongful act of any person or persons" does not appear in the Bulk Oil Clauses.

Clauses 5, 6, and 7—The Unseaworthiness and Unfitness Exclusion Clause and the War and Strikes Exclusion Clauses are the same as in the ICC.

Clause 8—Transit Clause

The definition of the duration of the risk is of importance on bulk oil for the following reasons:

a) Because of the number of losses that occur during the operation of loading and discharging cargo; and
b) Because the assessment of any claim for shortage necessarily starts with the determination of the quantity of cargo at the risk of the assured at the commencement of the coverage.

In short, the duration of the risk is from shore tank to shore tank, although provision is implicitly made for part of the transit to be performed by lighter vessels or vessels of smaller capacity than ocean tankers.

The term "leaves tanks for the purpose of loading" is deliberately broad enough to cover the movement of oil from one or more initial storage tanks in the tank farm at the place of loading into another tank or tanks for the purpose of loading onto ships.

The period of cutoff after the date of arrival of the vessel at the place of destination is thirty days, compared with sixty days, as provided in the ICC.

Clause 9—Termination of Contract of Carriage Clause

This clause is in the same terms as the corresponding clause in the ICC, except that in the event of the termination of the contract of carriage in the circumstances set out in the clause, and subject to prompt notice being given to the underwriters requesting a continuation of coverage, the period of time for which such extension may be granted (without any further extension being asked for) is thirty days, compared with the sixty days provided in the ICC.

Clauses 10 to 14 and 16 to 20, Plus One Note

Clauses 10 to 14, inclusive, and 16 to 20, inclusive, are the same as in the ICC, as is the footnote of the form.

THE MARINE INSURANCE HANDBOOK

Clause 15—Adjustment Clause

This clause had been designed to eliminate (as much as possible) claims for "paper loss," occurring as a result of the incompatibility of documents' recording quantities loaded and discharged, and the well-known difficulties of measuring liquid cargoes. A typical claim adjustment in accordance with the above clause would be as follows:

<u>Facts</u>

A quantity of 650,497 bbl. of crude oil is ascertained by meter readings to have been loaded from shore tanks to the vessel. A bill of lading was issued, based on shore tank figures, for 650,497 bbl. gross (650,157 bbl. net).

The consignment is insured for US$9,752,355 under the Institute Bulk Oil Clauses, with claims for shortages subject to a deductible of 0.50 percent on the whole shipment.

At destination, the quantity ascertained to have been discharged to shore tanks is 650,100 bbl.

Adjustment:

Received from shore tanks (gross)	650,497 bbl.
Delivered to shore tanks (gross)	645,100 bbl.
Short	5,397 bbl.
Less deductible 0.5 percent on whole shipment	3,252 bbl.
Claimed quantity short	2,145 bbl.

Insured value

If 650,497 bbl. are insured for US$9,752,355,
then 2,145 bbl. will insure for US$32,157

Occasional and Additional Clauses
4.3   Institute Malicious Damage Clause

In consideration of an additional premium, it is hereby agreed that the exclusion "deliberate damage to or deliberate destruction of the subject matter insured or any part thereof by the wrongful act of any person or persons" is deemed to be deleted, and further that this insurance covers loss or damage to the subject matter insured caused by malicious acts, vandalism, or sabotage, subject always to the other exclusions contained in this insurance."

The cover granted by this clause falls into two parts:

a) The exclusion (by clause 4.7 in the ICC (B) and (C)) of "deliberate damage to or deliberate destruction of the subject matter or any part thereof by the wrongful act of any person or persons" is deleted; and

b) Positive cover is granted against loss or damage caused by "malicious acts, vandalism, or sabotage."

The extension of cover granted by this clause will benefit an assured whose goods are covered under restricted conditions, but such extension will not be required when the goods are insured under "all risks" conditions.

A malicious act is one performed out of spite or ill will, or something of the like. By that definition, vandalism and sabotage are merely examples of malicious acts.

4.4 Institute Theft, Pilferage, and Nondelivery Clause
(For use with the Institute Clauses)

In consideration of an additional premium, it is agreed that this insurance covers loss of or damage to the subject matter insured caused by theft or pilferage or by nondelivery of an entire package, subject always to the exclusions contained in this insurance.

This additional clause will not be required by an assured who has taken out a policy on "all risks" conditions.

The additional risks open a question of whether three separate risks are covered by the clause or whether they are merely three different species of the same genus.

It may be argued that the context of the words "by theft or pilferage, or by nondelivery of an entire package" are considered to be of two separate perils insured: (1) theft or pilferage; and (2) nondelivery of an entire package. This construction is supported by the comma that appears after the word "pilferage," and by the repetition of the words "or by" before "nondelivery."

Following is a brief introduction to the clauses applied by companies for hull insurance to cover the risks that vessels may encounter from the stage of building until sailing in the seas or oceans.

CHAPTER 5

INSTITUTE TIME CLAUSES—HULLS, JANUARY 10, 1983

"This insurance is subject to English Law and Practice."

This condition is considered preferable to be retained in the clauses so that the appropriate court has the benefit of the wealth of English law and practice on marine insurance. The difference between the proper law of the contract and the correct jurisdiction was illustrated in the case of "Al Wahab," which went as far as the House of Lords. In this case, neither the plaintiffs nor the defendant insurers were English, and the policy had been issued in Kuwait. However, the policy form used the Lloyd's SG form of policy in accordance with the Marine Insurance Act of 1906, with the addition of standard Institute Clauses; the whole policy was in the English language. It was accepted by both sides that in Kuwait at the relevant time, there was no indigenous law of marine insurance. The House of Lords held:

1) It was not possible to interpret the policy or to determine what the mutual legal rights and obligations of the parties were except by reference to the Marine Insurance Act of 1906 and its substantive provisions; the English rules of conflict of laws applied, and the

proper law of the contract embodied in the policy was English law.

2) In the absence of an indigenous law of marine insurance in Kuwait, English law was the only system to which it was possible for a Kuwaiti court to give a sensible and precise meaning to the language that the parties had chosen to use in the policy.

3) Having no grounds for doubting that justice could be obtained in a Kuwaiti court, an English court could find no justification for compelling the defendants to submit to its jurisdiction.

5.1 Clause 1—Navigation

1. The clause makes it clear that the vessel is covered at all times, including while sailing or navigating with or without pilots, undertaking trial, and rendering assistance to other vessels or crafts in distress. However, it is warranted that the vessel shall not be towed, except when in need of assistance, and then only to the first safe port or place. This warranty does not exclude customary towage in or out of a port or dock, or in connection with loading and discharging.

2. The clause also stipulates that if cover is required for cargo loading or discharging operations at sea from or into another vessel, previous notice must be given to underwriters, as well as any amended terms of coverage and any additional premium agreed. The clause relates only to "trading operations" and not to cases of emergency following a casualty.

3. This clause deals with the situation in which a vessel sails with the intention of being broken up or sold for breaking up. In the absence of prior notice having been given to underwriters and other terms having been agreed upon, any claim for loss of or

damage to the vessel occurring subsequent to such sailing would be limited to the market value of the vessel as scrap at the time when the loss or damage is sustained.

5.2 Clause 2—Continuation

If, at the end of the period of insurance, the vessel is still short of its destination, it is held covered at a *pro rata* monthly premium until the destination is reached, provided that previous notice is given to underwriters.

5.3 Clause 3—Breach of Warranty

This clause provides for the breach of certain specified warranties to be held covered, subject to notice being given to underwriters immediately after receipt of advice and any amended terms and additional premium being agreed upon.

5.4 Clause 4—Termination

Any change in the vessel's classification status during the period of insurance is therefore an important matter for the insurers, and this clause provides for automatic termination of the coverage, in the absence of underwriters' written agreement to the contrary, at the time of the change of classification society or any change, suspension, discontinuation, withdrawal, or expiry of the vessel's class.

The insurance also terminates automatically in case of the change of ownership, transfer to new management, change of flag, charter on a bareboat basis, or requisition for title or use, unless underwriters have given their written agreement to the contrary.

Finally, the clause provides for a *pro rata* daily net return of premium in the event of automatic termination of the coverage.

5.5 Clause 5—Assignment

This clause outlines the steps that must be undertaken by the assured, and any subsequent assignors, before an assignment will be recognized by underwriters and become binding upon them. This is a reasonable precaution on the part of underwriters and enables them to ascertain that any claims are paid to the correct party.

5.6 Clause 6—Perils
5.6.1 Perils of the seas, rivers, lakes, or other navigable waters

The word "perils" denotes that something fortuitous and accidental is envisaged; incursion of sea water into the vessel does not necessarily amount to a loss by "perils of the seas." The policy covers accidents that may happen, not against events that must happen.

Although attempts have been made over the years, no one has successfully produced a complete definition of the expression "perils of the seas."

The term does not cover every accident or casualty that may happen to the subject matter insured. It must be a peril "of" the sea. Thus, in a court decision in which an insured vessel was blown over by a violent gust of wind while in graving dock, it was held not to be a loss by "perils of the seas." However, providing that the elements of fortuity and "of the sea" are present, violence of the weather is not an essential prerequisite; if, for example, a vessel becomes stranded on the coast in fair weather, or, as a result of negligence, is involved in a collision with another vessel, the resulting loss would be attributable to "perils of the seas."

5.6.2 Fire and explosion

The inclusion of both perils in the same clause is a logical and practical development. There is no explicit reference in the clauses to extinguishing damage; none is necessary under English law, which recognizes that any loss incurred to prevent a loss by an insured peril is recoverable as a loss by that peril.

5.6.3 Violent theft by persons from outside the vessel

Theft must be: (1) violent; and (2) performed by persons from outside the vessel.

The term does not cover clandestine theft or a theft committed by any one of the ship's company, whether by its crew or passengers. It has always been an accepted rule that simple theft is something that should be capable of prevention by the master, and as such, is not a proper subject for insurance under the marine policy.

5.6.4 Jettison

This term generally refers to the cargo that is jettisoned at a time of danger, but the vessel may be damaged as a result of such an operation, or (in extreme circumstances) part of the ship's equipment may be jettisoned.

5.6.5 Piracy

The term "pirates" denotes persons plundering indiscriminately for their own ends and not persons simply operating against the property of a particular state for a political end.

THE MARINE INSURANCE HANDBOOK

5.6.6 **Breakdown of, or accident to, nuclear installation or reactor**

In the event of contamination of an insured vessel by radioactive material (such as accidental emission from a nuclear power station), the cleanup costs would be recoverable as a reasonable cost of repairs.

5.6.7 **Contact with aircraft or similar objects falling therefrom; and conveyance, dock, or harbor equipment or installation**

This clause covers the risks of vessels being damaged by satellites running out of control and/or pieces of aircraft or space debris falling to earth.

5.6.8 **Earthquake, volcanic eruption, or lightning**

The clause adds coverage for cleaning of dust following volcanic eruption or lightning.

5.6.9 **Accidents in loading, discharging, or shifting cargo or fuel**

It is only the damage caused by accidents in the operations of loading, discharging, or shifting cargo or fuel that is covered. Damage suffered by the vessel as a result of cargo having been loaded into the vessel is not recoverable (such as damage to the hull plating from the loading and carriage of a corrosive cargo).

5.6.10 **Bursting of boilers, breaking of shafts, or any latent defect in the machinery or hull**

The policy covers "loss or damage to the subject matter insured caused by," and it is only the consequential damage that is covered, not the cost of repairing or replacing the latent defective parts. In the case of a boiler explosion or a shaft breakage, if there is no evidence that the original accident was caused by an insured peril, only the consequential damage would be recoverable, and there would be no claim for the cost of repairing or replacing the damaged boiler or shaft.

5.6.11 Negligence of master officers, crew, or pilots

It is only loss or damage caused by negligence of the master, officers, crew, or pilot that is covered, not the cost of the effects to work that should have been carried out by the crew.

5.6.12 Negligence of repairers or charterers, provided such repairers or charterers are not an assured hereunder

To file a claim under this clause, one must have evidence of physical loss or damage to the subject matter insured as a consequence of the repairers' or charterers' negligence.

5.6.13 Barratry of master officers or crew

The term "barratry" includes every willful act on the part of the master or crew of illegality, corruption, or criminal negligence, whereby the shipowner or the charters are prejudiced.

"Provided such loss or damage has not resulted from want of due diligence by the assured, owners, or managers."

The observation of due diligence is a question of fact in each individual case. Typical circumstances where the provision could be pleaded by the underwriters as a defense to a claim might be as follows:

(1) The bursting of a boiler that was found to have been beyond its due date for a Classification Society survey at the time of the casualty.

(2) A succession of crew negligence claims, where the evidence points to the crew employed being of insufficient caliber, perhaps coupled with inadequate management-control checks on the crew's performance by the owners or managers.

5.6.14 Masters, officers, crew, or pilots not to be considered owners (within the meaning of this clause, should they hold shares in the vessel)

Once it is accepted that an owner could combine the functions of owner and crew member, there is no other way of ascertaining the capacity in which he or she acted than by a comparison with what the position would have been if the ownership and crew membership were separated.

5.7 Clause 7—Pollution Hazard

The clause extends the insurance to cover loss of or damage to the vessel in the following circumstances:

1. The loss or damage must be caused by a governmental authority when acting to prevent or mitigate a real or threatened pollution hazard; and
2. The pollution hazard must result directly from damage to the vessel covered by the policy.

5.8 Clause 8—Three-Fourths Collision Liability

This was previously known as the "RDC" or "Running Down Clause." Forms of this clause have been in use since the early part of the nineteenth century. Its inclusion only became commonplace following a court decision in 1836, in which it was decided that under the ordinary form of the policy, underwriters were not liable for the balance that the insured vessel had to pay to the other when both were to blame for a collision. The clause had been subsequently refined over the years in light of court decisions, and in recent years, with the increasing importance and magnitude of the liabilities arising from consequential risks such as pollution, the clause had been recast to differentiate quite clearly between definitive coverage and the areas of exclusion, in particular those that are within the reach of the Protection and Indemnity Associations P&I cover.

Subject to the provisions of the clause, the underwriters agree to indemnify the assured for three-fourths of any sum or sums paid by the assured within the terms of the clause. The reason for coverage being limited to three-fourths is historical, as it was the original intention of underwriters when introducing the clause to encourage care on the part of the assured by insisting that one-fourth of the amount remain self-insured. The payment must arise "by reason of the assured becoming legally liable by way of damages," and the clause only covers liabilities arising out of tort. Such payment must be in consequence of the vessel insured "coming into collision with any other vessel." What constitutes a collision with another "ship or vessel" has been the subject of several judicial decisions.

Relevant Court Cases:

(i) An insured vessel collided with a pontoon crane, which was permanently moored to a riverbank in a naval dockyard. It was held that the pontoon was not a ship or vessel, as its primary purpose was to float and lift, and not to navigate.
(ii) An insured vessel ran into a barge that was lying half-submerged following a recent collision with another vessel; this was held to be a collision within the terms of the policy.

(iii) A collision occurred with a vessel that had been sunk and was lying at the bottom of the sea, but salvage operations were at hand, and the salvers had a reasonable expectation of raising it. This was held to be a collision with a ship or vessel within the terms of the Collision Clause.

The indemnity for collision liability is in addition to the indemnity provided by the other terms and conditions of the insurance, but it limits an underwriters' total liability to three-fourths of the insured value in any one collision. This means that, regardless of any other claim, the limit of liability for any claim under clause 8 would be three-fourths of the insured value.

The clause imports the principle of cross-liability into the adjustment of claims under the clause. When two vessels are in collision and both are to blame, the respective liabilities are assessed, a setoff then occurs, and there is a single payment by the vessel with the balance to pay. This is known as a single liability.

In addition, the underwriters agree to pay three-fourths of the legal costs involved in testing liability or in limiting liability, provided that they were incurred with the prior written consent of underwriters.

5.9   Clause 9—Sistership

If two vessels under the same ownership are in collision, there is no tortious liability between the two ships due to the fact that a person cannot bring an action against himself. If both vessels are insured, the shipowner can claim for the physical damage under his or her policies, subject to two policy deductibles.

By this clause, the assured is placed in the same position when the insured vessel is in collision or receives salvage services from a vessel that belonged to entirely different owners. The clause also deals with the procedural manner in which the liability for the collision or the amount payable for the salvage services is to be assessed.

5.10   Clause 10—Notice of Claim and Tenders
5.10.1   Clause 10.1
This clause stipulates that when an accident giving rise to a potential claim has occurred, notice should be given to the underwriters, or where appropriate, to the nearest Lloyd's agents. This enables the underwriters to obtain an early indication of the extent of the damage, and the initial survey is also an ideal opportunity to obtain much of the evidence regarding the accident.

5.10.2   Clause 10.2
Under clause 10.2, underwriters have the right to decide to which port the vessel should proceed for the damage dry-docking and/or repair, and they reserve the right of veto concerning the place of repair or repairing firm. When underwriters elect to nominate a port of repair, they agree to refund to the assured the additional expense of the voyage arising from compliance with their instructions.

5.10.3   Clause 10.3
This clause gives underwriters the right to take tenders or to require further tenders to be taken. When underwriters invoke their rights under this clause, an allowance is payable by underwriters at the rate of 30 percent per annum on the insured value.

5.11 Clause 11—General Average And Salvage
5.11.1 Clause 11.1
Under clause 11.1, the coverage is against only the vessel's proportion of salvage, salvage charges, and/or general average, which should be differentiated from the proportion of loss that falls upon the shipowner.

5.11.2 Clause 11.2
Hull underwriters agree to the adjustment of general average according to either the York/Antwerp rules, or, in the absence of any special terms, in the contract of affreightment, according to the law and practice in place at the destination where the venture ends.

5.12 Clause 12—Deductible
In order to determine whether one deductible or more should be applied in the case of an accident or occurrence, a special committee was formed, and it was agreed that:

1. One deductible is to be applied when either:
   a) There is only one accident or occurrence from which the claims arise; or
   b) Even though there is more than one accident or occurrence, these accidents or occurrences are not separate, but they instead form a connected set of events from which the claims arise.
2. On the other hand, if one or more of the events from which the claims arise are the result of a new cause and are not directly connected with the previous events (such as that which would be considered by law as a new, intervening cause), then more than one deductible is to be applied to the claims.

The committee recognized that, in practice, the determination of the number of deductibles to be applied will depend upon a close consideration of the facts in each case.

No deductible would be applied to a claim for a total or constructive total loss.

In regard to the cost of sighting the bottom after a stranding, even if no damage is found, provided that the expense was reasonably incurred especially for that purpose, any claim thereunder is payable without application of the policy deductible.

Clause 12.2 stipulates that all heavy weather (or ice) occurring during a single sea passage between two successive ports shall be treated as due to one accident. There is also detailed provision for the apportionment of the deductible when heavy weather or ice extends over a period not wholly covered by the insurance.

Example:

A vessel encountered floating ice during one passage, over the period December 20, 2015 to January 10, 2016. The relevant policies applied for the period of twelve months commencing January 1, 2015 (a deductible of US$6,000) and January 1, 2016 (a deductible of $12,000). The number of days of floating ice recorded in the vessel's deck logbook amount to five, two of which occurred in 2015 and three in 2016 (there are no specific areas of damage recorded on any of the days in question).

The total cost of repairs amounted to $10,000.

The claim and deductibles were as follows:

2015 Policy Year

	Claim
Cost of repair	$10,000
Of which apply to this policy two-fifths	$4,000
Less policy deductible two-fifths x $6,000	$2,400
	$1,600

2016 Policy Year

	Claim
Cost of repair	$10,000
Of which apply to this policy three-fifths	$6,000
Less deductible three-fifths x $ 12,000	$7,200
	No Claim

Recoveries

This occurs when, by reason of the application of the policy deductible, the amount paid by the underwriters is less than an indemnity. In English practice, in the absence of any policy provision to the contrary, the process is to divide the amount recovered ratably between the assured and the insurers in proportion to the net claim paid by the insurers and the policy deductible borne by the assured.

5.13 Clause 13—Duty of Assured (Sue and Labor)
"In case of any loss or misfortune…"

As a result of the operation of insured perils, the subject matter of the insurance has been brought into such danger that, without unusual or extraordinary labor and/or expense, a loss will probably fall on the underwriters.

"It is the duty of the assured and their servants and agents to take such measures as may be reasonable…"

This imposes a firm duty upon the assured and their agents to take such measures as may be reasonable (and necessary) under this clause.

Only those expenses that are incurred by the assured, their servants, or agents are recoverable under the clause.

"For the purpose of averting or minimizing a loss that would be recoverable under this insurance…"

In considering whether the measures undertaken were for the purpose of averting or minimizing a loss that would be recoverable under the insurance, (1) the peril must be one that is covered by the policy, and (2) there must have been the danger of a loss that would have been covered by the policy, so that if the only danger had been a partial loss under a policy that covered total loss only, there would be no claim for any sue and labor expenses.

"General average salvage charges and collision defense or attack cost are not recoverable under this clause."

General average losses and contributions and salvage charges are not recoverable under the suing and laboring clause.

Clause 13.3 makes it clear that if the assured or the underwriters undertake any measures with the object of saving, protecting, or recovering the insured property, such measures

THE MARINE INSURANCE HANDBOOK

shall not be considered as a waiver or acceptance of abandonment and shall not be allowed to prejudice the rights of either party.

5.14 Clause 14—New for Old

Claims payable without deduction new for old.

When old parts of the vessel that have been lost or damaged through the operation of insured perils are replaced by new parts, there is an element of betterment. For many years, hull insurances have provided for claims to be payable without being subject to "new for old" deductions.

5.15 Clause 15—Bottom Treatment

This clause is, by necessity, of a fairly technical nature, and the adjustment of any claims thereunder is generally left to the average adjuster and his or her technical consultants.

5.16 Clause 16—Wages and Maintenance

The wages and maintenance of the crew may, under certain circumstances, be allowed in general average, in which event a ship's proportion may form a claim under clause 11 (General Average and Salvage). Regarding whether there is any liability under English law for wages and maintenance of the crew as part of a claim for particular average, the practice had evolved for appropriate allowances. Such payments are calculated in a particular average for either the whole or part of the crew on removal passages, and while engaged in such practices as docking and undocking the vessel, and acting as shipkeepers during average repairs.

The present wording of the clause states:

"No claim shall be allowed other than in general average, for wages and maintenance of the master, officers, and crew."

The exclusion only relates to the wages and maintenance and would not preclude a claim for overtime and/or special payments to the crew in appropriate circumstances, for example, assisting on damage repairs or tank cleaning. The terms "wages and maintenance" and "crew" are defined as:

(a) Wages

The term "wages" comprises the gross amount of all those payments made by the shipowner to the members of the crew on a monthly, weekly, or other periodic basis, including leave pay, overseas allowances, and so forth.

(b) Maintenance

The term "maintenance"comprises the cost of provisions (such as laundry and so forth) for the crew, together with the cost of providing accommodation onshore in certain circumstances.

(c) Crew

This term comprises those members of the ship's complement of seagoing rank engaged under articles and/or entered in the master's portage bill or harbor wage account.

"Except when incurred solely for the necessary removal of the vessel from one port to another for repair of damage covered by the underwriters…"

It should be noted that the limitation to the exclusion only applies when the wages and maintenance have been incurred solely for the necessary removal of the vessel for damage repairs. Thus, if the removal was for both average and owners' repairs, no wages and maintenance are, in practice, paid by underwriters under this clause.

"Or for trial trips for such repairs…"

For example, if, following main-engine damage that forms a claim under the policy, the vessel goes out for a trial trip, the wages and maintenance of the crew for the period while underway on trial will be claimable.

"And then only for such wages and maintenance as are incurred while the vessel is underway…"

An allowance can only be made for the period while the vessel is actually underway, so that any period spent at anchor outside a port, for example, would be excluded.

5.17 Clause 17—Agency Commission

The intention of underwriters is to exclude all claims for remuneration by the assured, or by their managers, or agents for time and trouble incurred on any aspect of a claim. The clause does not exclude the fees and charges of an agent at a port of call, which can still be recoverable under certain circumstances, with the other port charges as part of the cost of repair.

5.18 Clause 18—Unrepaired Damage

The measure of indemnity for unrepaired damage is limited to the estimated reasonable cost of repairs if this figure is less than the depreciation in the market value of the vessel.

In the event of a subsequent total loss, any unrepaired damage becomes merged into the total loss, and the assured has lost nothing by reason of the unrepaired damage.

Underwriters' overall limit of liability in respect to unrepaired damage is the insured value of the vessel at the time when the insurance terminates.

5.19 Clause 19—Constructive Total Loss
5.19.1 Clause 19.1

This clause contains the express provision that the insured value shall be taken as the repaired value. It is the insured value that forms the point of reference when determining whether the vessel is a constructive total loss and against which the estimated cost of repairing the damage must be compared.

When the cost of recovery and/or repair of the vessel exceeds the insured value, the assured has the choice of either claiming a constructive total loss or, alternatively, the assured may exercise his or her option of repairing the vessel and claiming 100 percent partial loss.

In assessing the cost of recovery or repair, only the cost relating to a single accident or sequence of damages arising from the same accident may be taken into account.

5.20 Clause 20—Freight Waiver

Underwriters give up their rights to any freight in the course of being earned when the vessel is a total or constructive total loss, so that it remains the property of the shipowner.

5.21 Clause 21—Disbursements Warranty

The disbursements clause was introduced with the aim of limiting the amount of such ancillary insurance that can be affected. The clause limits the sum of all of such additional insurance, not to exceed 25 percent of the insured value.

The clause lists the additional insurances that are permitted. These limits are related to the sums insured. In practice, the assured has the choice (subject to the rules of insurable interest) of apportioning the 25 percent additional insurance allowed between the different types of insurance, as set fourth in the clause, as he or she sees fit and to suit his or her individual circumstances.

5.22   Clause 22—Return for Lay-Up and Cancelation

The clause provides for a return of the premium in two circumstances:

1. If the insurance is canceled by agreement, a return is due of the *pro rata* monthly premium for each uncommenced month.
2. If the vessel is laid up in a port or in a lay-up area approved by the underwriters, a return of premium is due for each period of thirty consecutive days at the specified rates, which should be entered into the clause, different rates applying depending on whether the vessel is under repair or otherwise.

The returns are subject to the following provisions:

a) If a total loss of the vessel occurs during the period of the policy, no return of premium is due.
b) In no case shall a return be allowed when the vessel is lying in exposed or unprotected waters.
c) The loading or discharging of operations or the presence of cargo onboard will not prejudice the return of the premium.

d) If the annual rate of premium is adjusted, the rates of return should also be adjusted accordingly.

5.23 Clauses 23, 24, 25—War, Strikes, and Malicious-Acts Exclusions

Both piracy and barratry can result in the "seizure or arrest, restraint, or detainment of the vessel." Examples of this would be seizure of a vessel by pirates or the impounding of a vessel by customs authorities following smuggling by the crew. It is for this reason that the exclusion of claims caused by capture, arrest, restraint, or detainment is expressed to be "barratry and piracy."

The clause excludes claims resulting from derelict mines, torpedoes, or other weapons of war.

To apply the malicious-act exclusion, it is necessary to establish that a claim arises from the detonation of an explosion or any weapons of war and that it was caused by a person acting maliciously or from a political motive.

A claim resulting from the accidental explosion of a cargo of explosives will not be affected by the exclusion.

5.24 Clause 26—Nuclear Exclusion

This exclusion is universally found in insurance policies.

CHAPTER 6

INSTITUTE TIME CLAUSES—HULLS: RESTRICTED CONDITIONS

Not all shipowners require insurance on full conditions; the saving in premium obtained by opting for restricted conditions may be the governing factor. For older vessels, the shipowner may have no choice if underwriters are not willing to offer insurance on full conditions.

The main types of restricted conditions available in the market include:

6.1 Institute Time Clauses—Hulls (Total Loss, General Average, and Three-Fourths Collision Liability)
(Including Salvage, Salvage Charges, and Sue and Labor)

The cover is expressed to be against only "total loss" (actual or constructive) of the subject matter insured. The assured is also covered for any proportion of salvage, salvage charges, and/or general average attaching to the vessel.

6.2 Institute Time Clauses—Hulls (Total Loss Only)
(Including Salvage, Salvage Charges, and Sue and Labor)

Cover is expressed to be against only "total loss (actual or constructive) of the subject matter insured."

Collision liabilities are not covered under these clauses.

6.3 Institute Voyage Clauses—Hulls

In the early days of insurance, all policies were for a round voyage; the reverse is now the case, and the vast majority of insurances are effected on a time basis. For the minority of cases (in which insurance is required for a voyage), two sets of main clauses are available.

6.3.1 Institute Voyage Clauses—Hulls

1. Navigation

The nature of the voyage is one of the material facts that must be disclosed before the contract is concluded. The underwriters in voyage insurance have ample opportunity to impose any special conditions considered necessary at the time of initial negotiations for the placing of the risk.

2. Change of voyage

This clause replaces the continuation clause in the ITC—Hulls, which would not be relevant to voyage insurance.

The change of voyage clause ameliorates the position under English law very substantially and holds the assured covered in cases of deviation or change of voyage or any breach of warranty as to towage or salvage services. This is subject to the provision that the assured gives notice to underwriters immediately when he or she becomes aware of the facts, and that any amended terms of coverage and additional premium are agreed upon.

The Institute Voyage Clauses do not include Clause 3—Breach of Warranty and Clause 4—Termination, which appear in the institute time clauses (Hull), as they are not relevant to voyage insurance.

6.4 Institute Voyage Clauses—Hulls: Total Loss, General Average, and Three-Fourths Collision Liability (Including Salvage, Salvage Charges, and Sue and Labor)

The change is only in the Perils Clause 4, which covers inter alia.

4.1 This insurance covers total loss (actual or constructive) of the subject matter insured caused by the list of perils as per ITC—Hull.

6.5 Additional Insurance for Shipowners

History

One of the oldest principles in marine insurance is that the subject of insurance will be covered for the value that it has at the commencement of the risk. In the early days, underwriters might require some proof that the value that they were called upon to insure was realistic. The proof that the shipowners could disclose were the bills for the amounts paid for the ships, their fitting out, and the monies that had been disbursed in anticipation of the projected venture.

Section 16(1) of the Marine Insurance Act of 1906 gives this old rule:

"In insurance on a ship, the insurable value is the value at the commencement of the risk, of the ship, including its outfit, provisions, and stores for the officers and crew, money advanced for seamen's wages, and other disbursements (if any) incurred to make the ship fit for the voyage or venture contemplated by the policy, plus the charges of insurance upon the whole."

That is, there was an insurable interest for the outlays made upon the commencement of the voyage, and upon which the shipowner expected to make a profit. It was seen that if, during the voyage, the shipowner had to disburse additional sums by way of refitting the ship, engaging new members of the crew, and taking on further provisions, those expenditures would also become proper subjects for insurance.

Hence, the need to take out additional insurance by way of "disbursements," or, if the ship should have an enhanced value by reason of its being engaged for a special trade, upon its "increased value."

Consequently, the shipowner was glad to have the facility of obtaining further insurance when necessary, by way of disbursements or increased value.

6.5.1 Excess Liabilities

It is common practice for shipowners to take out supplementary insurance on "excess liabilities" to enable them, in the event of the vessel being undervalued in hull policies, to obtain further coverage for the excess of any specified contributions or liabilities over and above the amounts recoverable under their hull policies.

6.5.2 Disbursements and Increased Value (Total Loss Only, including Excess Liabilities)

Insurance coverage is to include the following:

I. Disbursements and increased value, the sum insured being payable only in the event of the vessel being settled under the hull policy as a total or constructive total loss.
II. Excess Liabilities

6.5.3 Extended Conditions (Institute Additional Perils Clauses—Hulls)

This clause is designed to provide an extension of coverage subject to the payment of additional premium.

The extended perils to be covered include the cost of repairing or replacing any boiler that has burst, any shaft that has broken, or any latently defective part that has caused loss or damage covered by clause 6.2.2 of the ITC Hulls.

The coverage also includes loss of or damage to the vessel caused "by negligence, incompetence, or error of judgment of any person whatsoever." The intention of the clause is that parts that are or have become defective as a result of a fault or error in design or construction will only be paid for if there is a failure or breakdown in service, resulting in consequential damage. The part will not be paid for if it has been condemned in anticipation of failure or breakdown, or if it is simply found to be defective without any other damage having been caused.

6.5.4 Additional Deductibles for Machinery Damage

The intention is that this should only be incorporated into policies covering vessels or fleets. The clause reads:

"Notwithstanding any provision to the contrary in this insurance, a claim for loss or damage to any machinery, shaft, electric equipment, or wiring, boiler condenser heating coil, or associated pipe work, arising from any of the perils enumerated in clause 6.2.2 to 6.2.5 inclusive of the Institute Time Clauses—Hulls or from fire or explosion when either has originated in a machinery space, shall be subject to a deductible of ___. Any balance remaining, after application of this deductible, with any other claim arising from the same accident or occurrence, shall then be subject to the deductible in clause 12.1 of the ITC—Hulls.

The figure for the additional deductible has to be agreed upon at the time of effecting the insurance and then has to be entered into the clause.

Before the additional deductible comes into operation, the following requirements must be met:

(I) The claim must be for "loss or damage" to any of the enumerated parts of the vessel.
(II) To any machinery, shaft, electrical equipment, or wiring, boiler condenser, heating oil, or associated pipe work.
(III) Arising from any of the perils enumerated in clauses 6.2.2 to 6.2.5, inclusive of the ITC—Hulls, or from fire or explosion when either has originated in a machinery space.

6.5.5 Freight Insurance

Schedule 1 of the Marine Insurance Act of 1906 defines "freight" as follows:

"The term 'freight' includes a profit derivable by a shipowner from the employment of his or her ship to carry his or her own goods or movables, as well as freight payable by a third party, but does not include passage money."

The charterer or cargo owner may well have an insurable interest in advance freight, insofar as it is not repayable in case of loss. Such advances of freight are not intended to be the subject of insurance on the Institute Freight Clauses and are more properly covered as part of the cargo.

6.6 War and Strikes Risks Forms

Maritime ventures were of high risk during the days of drafting the old Lloyd's hull policy forms. The risks are not limited to the navigation and natural perils but also more hazardous perils regarding war, warlike operations, and hostile acts. In those days, every merchantperson was armed, and the gunner was as important a member of the crew as the boatswain. Even so, a heavily laden merchantperson was no match, either in sailing ability or firepower, for a man-of-war or a pirate cutter, and many were the losses that underwriters had to bear from those causes in the seventeenth and eighteenth centuries.

6.6.1 Institute War and Strikes Clauses, Hulls—Time

The policy form combines war risks and strikes risks in one document, and the following words appear in the heading: "This insurance is subject to English law and practice."

6.6.1.1 *Perils*

The coverage includes the risk of "war civil, war revolution, rebellion, insurrection, or civil strife arising therefrom or any hostile act by or against a belligerent power" in clause 1.1 as appears in the Institute War Clauses—Cargo.

Clause 1.2 is broader than the corresponding clause in the Institute War Clauses—Cargo, as the perils of capture, seizure, restraint, or detainment are not limited to those that arise in consequence of the war and warlike risks set out in clause 1.1.

Subject to the list of exclusions, a seizure, arrest, or restraint exercised in time of peace by the political or executive arm of a government or power will be covered, equally with such acts performed in war or warlike circumstances.

Clause 1.5 adds the risk of loss or damage of persons "acting maliciously." "Maliciously" is defined as "out of spite," and as an insured peril, it may well overlap with acts performed with political motivation or in the course of a civil commotion. Sabotage is a malicious act. So are many acts of barratry, but as barratry is one of the perils insured under the Institute Time Clauses—Hulls, a loss from this clause will be excluded from the war and strikes cover unless the act of barratry involved the detonation of an explosive, in which event it would be excluded from the marine risks.

"Confiscation or Expropriation"

These perils, which appear in clause 1.6, are not more than kinds of political or executive acts of a government or a power that are comprehended within the words "arrest, restraints, and detainments of all kings, princes, and people," as they appear in the old Lloyd's form of policy.

The definition of "confiscation" is as follows:

"Appropriation to the public treasury (by way of penalty), with the additional colloquial meaning of 'legal robbery with the sanction of ruling power.'"

"Expropriation" suggests an executive act of dispossession, not necessarily by way of a penalty.

6.6.1.2 *Incorporation*
This clause incorporates the relevant provision of the Institute Time Clauses—Hulls, particularly those relating to General Average and Salvage, Sue and Labor Charges, and the clauses

dealing with the adjustment of claims. It is to be noted that in one respect, the coverage granted by the Institute War and Strikes Clauses—Hulls Time is broader than that which is provided by the Institute Time Clauses. This is in respect to collision liability, which is granted in full (four-fourths).

6.6.1.3 *Detainment*

By section 60(2) of the Marine Insurance Act of 1906, there is a constructive total loss in which the assured is deprived of the possession of his or her ship by a peril insured against, and it is unlikely that he or she can recover it. During the outbreak of war between Iraq and Iran, a number of ships were trapped in the Shatt-Al-Arab by the outbreak of hostilities, and even those that were physically able to sail were prohibited from so doing by the Iraqi authorities. While clearly subject to restraint, underwriters questioned whether the assured had been deprived of the possession of their ships, and if they had, whether they were likely or unlikely to recover them. A test case, the "Bamburi," was selected for the arbitration of a judge, who found in favor of the claimants. The arbitrator dealt with the following points:

(i) The arbitrator found that detention of the vessel proximately was caused by perils insured.
(ii) Owners had been deprived of possession.
(iii) It was unlikely that the owners could recover the vessel (within a reasonable time).

6.6.1.4 *Exclusions*

Clause 4.1.1 reproduces the Nuclear Weapon exclusion, which is also found in the ITC—Hulls.

Clause 4.1.2 excludes any claim arising from the outbreak of war involving any two or more of the major powers. In this case, even the insurance is also automatically terminated.

Clause 4.1.3 excludes "requisition or preemption." The term "requisition" means a demand for use in military service. "Preemption" is understood to have something of the same meaning as it does in the United States of America. In either case, it is presumed that the owner will lose possession only for a temporary period of time and will have the vessel returned to him or her by the requisitioning authority when it is no longer required. It is also to be noted that requisition is one of the events that brings about the automatic termination of the insurance.

Clause 4.1.4 excludes the perils of capture, seizure, and so forth (including confiscation or expropriation) by the government or a public or local authority of the country in which the vessel is owned or registered.

Clause 4.1.5 excludes arrest and like actions (including confiscation or expropriation) arising under quarantine regulations or by reason of infringement of any customs or trading regulations.

Clause 4.1.6 excludes the operation of ordinary judicial processes, and those other circumstances that give rise to the vessel being placed under civil arrest at the suit of an aggrieved party.

Clause 4.1.7 excludes "piracy," which is accepted as a marine risk.

Clause 4.2 is inserted in order to avoid any duplication of cover with the ITC—Hulls.

Clause 4.3 is designed to prevent any claim falling upon the policy containing the Institute War and Strikes Clauses, which can or could be recovered under other insurance on the vessel. In the event of there being such a duplication of coverage, it is intended that the other insurance should pay on a "first loss" basis.

Clause 4.4 excludes any claim for expense arising from delay, except when allowable in general average.

Clause 5—Termination

Clause 5.1 permits either party to give the other seven days' notice before the cancelation becomes effective. The underlying intention of the clause is to enable underwriters to vary the rate of premium and/or the conditions of the insurance in the event of a serious change of circumstances relating to war risks in the vessel's likely trading area.

The second part of the clause relates to the reinstatement of the insurance if underwriters and the assured can agree to the new terms within the period of the seven days' notice.

Clause 5.2 relating to automatic termination is self-explanatory.

There is also an important caution at the foot of the clauses, which reads as follows:

"This insurance shall not become effective if, subsequent to its acceptance by the underwriters and prior to the intended time of attachment, there has occurred any event that would have automatically terminated this insurance under the provisions of clause 5 above."

CHAPTER 7

REINSURANCE

7.1 Principles of reinsurance

Principles of reinsurance are namely these:

1. Insurable interest
2. Indemnity
3. Utmost good faith
4. Legality

The insurance effected by an insurer to cover wholly or in part the risk he or she has undertaken is legal, and the principle of "utmost good faith" is to be observed by the reinsured and the reinsurer in the same manner as practiced by the direct insurer vis-à-vis the insured. The principle of indemnity may not to work perfectly in reinsurance practice as it is in the direct insurance, due to the predetermined limits usually agreed upon between the two parties in any reinsurance agreement (treaty).

7.2 Purpose

The main purpose that may be quoted for an insurer to put a reinsurance agreement into effect is to spread the risk. This fact is applicable for all types of reinsurance in which the ceding company looks to stabilize its claim ratio as well as its financial standings.

7.3 Definition

A treaty of reinsurance is a contract whereby the reinsurer agrees to reinsure the whole or a part of a specific class or classes of risks to be underwritten by the reassured (original insurer). Schedules giving particulars of the risks underwritten are usually forwarded periodically to the reinsurers.

7.4 Methods

Major methods of reinsurance are *proportional* and *nonproportional* contracts. They can be transacted on *facultative* or *treaty* bases.

7.4.1 Proportional Reinsurance

1.1.1.1 Facultative Reinsurance

"Facultative" means optional, the power to act according to a free choice. That is, the reinsurance underwriter is free to accept or decline each proposition, and the insurer is not compelled to cede, as he or she is bound to a reinsurance treaty.

1.1.1.2 Treaty Reinsurance

There are basically two main types of proportional treaty reinsurance.

First, there is a Quota Share Treaty, which meets the requirement of small and newly founded insurance companies. The treaty is designed to share the gross retention of the ceding company between itself and the reinsurers. In brief, a preagreed percentage is applied with a limit per acceptance; that is, a 40/60 percent quota share treaty with a limit of \$100,000 of any one risk (any one policy) means that the sum insured up to the said limit will be shared between the two parties (US$40,000 by the ceding company and $60,000 by the reinsurer). Consequently, claims will also be shared accordingly.

The second type of proportional treaty reinsurance is called the Surplus Treaty system, which enables the ceding company to accept larger sums insured than its gross retention, the surplus being ceded to the reinsurers.

The capacity of a surplus treaty is always a multiple of the ceding company's gross or net retention. A gross retention is that which is retained by the ceding company and its quota share reinsurance, whereas the net retention is that amount retained by the ceding company alone.

Example 1:

A company fixes its retention to be $100,000 for its marine cargo business and effects a first surplus treaty for ten lines and a second surplus treaty for five lines. The company writes policies with sum insured of $90,000, $100,000, $500,000, $750,000, $1,000,000, $1,500,000, $1,600,000, and $1,750,000. The distribution in accordance with the arranged treaties will be as follows:

Policy	Sum Insured	Retention	1st Surplus	2nd Surplus	Balance
1	90,000	90,000	-	-	-
2	100,000	100,000	-	-	-
3	500,000	100,000	400,000	-	-
4	750,000	100,000	650,000	-	-
5	1,000,000	100,000	900,000	-	-
6	1,500,000	100,000	900,000	500,000	-
7	1,600,000	100,000	900,000	500,000	100,000
8	1,750,000	100,000	900,000	500,000	250,000

The above examples show where the treaty had been filled to its capacity for the first six risks, but the seventh and eighth had balances not covered under the agreement. Therefore, the solution is either to retain the balance amount or to seek a facultative reinsurance to accept them.

7.4.2 Facultative Obligatory Reinsurance

This contract combines the principles of both the facultative and the treaty methods of proportional reinsurance. Under a facultative obligatory treaty, the ceding company is not obliged to cede to its reinsurers risks falling within the scope of the treaty. However, where it chooses to do so, reinsurers are obliged to accept the cession. This demonstrates that the facultative obligatory is operating like a surplus treaty.

This type of treaty is often arranged to provide additional capacity for long- and well-experienced underwriters who have good records with their reinsurers and are known to write only first-class risks. This type is usually written with a lower percentage of commission as compared to other treaties.

7.4.3 Nonproportional Treaties

The various methods of nonproportional reinsurance are based on the concept of agreed limit to be retained by the cedant and other reinsurers to accept up to an agreed limit. Accordingly, the direct insurer will pay claims up to a certain limit without the participation of the reinsurer, but in a case in which the loss exceeds the retained limit, the reinsurer will pay his or her share up to the agreed capacity.

The amount assumed per loss by the cedant is known as the deductible, the first loss, or the priority. The reinsurer's part of the loss is known as the cover.

Example:

Consider a company that writes fire risks and decides to meet any claim up to $50,000. The company's maximum exposure per risk is US$250,000; therefore, it requires a nonproportional treaty for the excess of the $50,000 (which is $200,000).

This treaty will be expressed as being of $200,000 in excess of $50,000.

The following illustration shows the distribution of three separate claims of $40,000, $150,000, and $275,000 that fall under the treaty:

Claim	Cedant share	Reinsurer Share	Balance
40,000	40,000	-	-
150,000	50,000	100,000	-
275,000	50,000	200,000	25,000

It is noted that the cover is not sufficient to meet the third loss and a balance of $25,000, which will fall on the account of the cedant company.

7.4.4 Excess of Loss Treaty

The ceding company in the above example had decided to accept a loss up to $50,000 but in case of accumulation of losses as a consequence of hurricane, earthquake, or major fire, the direct insurer may be exposed to a loss for a specific occurrence or event that exceeds protection.

A solution could be to arrange an Excess of Loss treaty, which is either

a) per risk cover or
b) per event cover.

Both covers are normally placed in layers, with a specified limit for the ceding company and the reinsurer.

Definition of Event:

The definition of one event varies in accordance with the type of insurance. In product liability, the *event* giving rise to a claim may be construed as the act of manufacturing the faulty product or the moment at which injury was caused.

In earthquake insurance, the initial earth tremor may be followed by a number of minor tremors spread over a week or more; the definition of an event is to be specifically determined and may include an "hour's clause," which is normally added in the coverage that involves natural perils.

In marine insurance, the problem regarding a definition of event has largely concerned war risks. It is difficult to predict the type or length of a conflict; therefore, an excess of loss contract on an event basis must be described as an imperfect method of reinsurance.

7.5 Treaty Wording

A treaty is a signed agreement that evidences a contract of treaty reinsurance between the parties. The wording should be clear in expression and should avoid ambiguity. Proportional and nonproportional wording differs in concept and conditions.

The main features of both treaties are as follows:

1) Business Clause
2) Business Covered
3) Territorial Scope
4) Treaty Details
5) Attachment of Cession and Termination of Treaty

6) Exclusions
7) Commission
8) Accounting Details
    a) Periodical Accounts
    b) Losses: Advice and Settlement
9) Premium Reserve Deposit
10) Loss Reserve Deposit
11) Currency
12) Profit Commission

CHAPTER 8

GENERAL AVERAGE

General Average is a concept that is specific to maritime transport and has its origin in the earliest days of seaborne trade. The basic principle was recognized by seafaring nations in similar terms: any sacrifice of property, such as jettison, or any extraordinary expenditure that is made for the common safety of ship and cargo is contributed to by the surviving property on the basis of arrived values. In the eighteenth century, divergence between English and European or US law and practice in the application of this principle became a serious inconvenience to commercial interests. From 1860 onward, there was a concerted international effort toward greater uniformity, culminating in the York-Antwerp Rules of 1890, which became operative by insertion into contracts of carriage.

Regular revision of the rules was carried by the Committee Maritime International (CMI). The CMI is a nongovernmental international organization dedicated to the unification of maritime law in all aspects, and which is made up of National Maritime Law Associations.

The York-Antwerp Rules recognize two main types of allowances:

1. "Common safety" allowance: This is a sacrifice of property (such as flooding a cargo hold to fight a fire) or expenditure (such as salvage or lightening a vessel) that was made or incurred while the ship and cargo were in the grip of peril. Since the early nineteenth century, English law and practice have largely recognized only this category of General Average.

2. "Common benefit" allowance: Once a vessel was at a port of refuge, European countries and the United States generally viewed expenses necessary to enable the ship to resume the voyage safely (but not the cost of repairing accidental damage to the ship) as also being General Average. This included, for example, the cost of discharging, storing, and reloading cargo as necessary to do repairs, and pay out port charges and wages. The concept is subject to rules to govern the system on application and adjustment of contributions as per the following rules.

8.1 General Average And York-Antwerp Rules

Introduction: The word "average" means a "loss" in shipping matters. Therefore, "particular average" means a partial loss in marine insurance. The term "general average" refers to a system whereby some losses are shared between the participants in a marine venture.

Origin: General average is as old as the oldest commercial sea voyages and is a natural law of the sea founded on equity. Historical records tell us that the system of general average (GA), involving a contribution from the interests involved in a maritime venture, has been in existence since the earliest days of seaborne traffic. The object of the system was to encourage shipmasters and others who sailed with them to make exertions to ensure safety whenever a peril threatened the joint venture.

8.2 General Average in English Law

The statutory definition of GA appears in section 66 of the MIA of 1906, reading:

"A general average loss is a loss caused by or is a direct consequence of a general average act. It includes a general average expenditure as well as a general average sacrifice.

There is a general average act, where any extraordinary sacrifice or expenditure is voluntarily and reasonably made or incurred in time of peril for the purpose of preserving the property imperiled in the common venture."

The general average therefore denotes a calculation whereby the general average sacrifice or expenditure is properly assessed and is shared ratably among cargo owners, shipowners, and charterers (if any), whose interest must be precisely evaluated for the purpose.

8.3 Main Features of the General Average Definition

Extraordinary: General average applies when there is an extraordinary occurrence. This is an essential part of the definition of general average. It is not only the risk or peril faced in the voyage that should be extraordinary but that the measures adopted to meet it should also be so. Therefore, if a vessel goes aground and uses extra fuel to right itself, that which is accountable in general average is the difference between the ordinary daily consumption and the actual fuel incurred during the procedure.

Peril: The sacrifice or expenditure must be made or incurred in respect to a real danger.

Reasonableness: The expenditure must be reasonably made or incurred.

Voluntariness: It is a voluntary, deliberate, or intentional act.

Success: General average is payable because the sacrifice or expenditure made or incurred benefited the rest of the marine venture. The unsuccessful act cannot amount to a general average.That is , if the ship in peril was flooded with sea watr and expenditure incurred to reloat her but failed ,the act is not successful and not within the defitionion of general average.

Fault: If the interest owing the contribution can establish that there was some fault in the general average, which could be raised by the debtor, then a claim is enforceable against the party who is liable for the fault. For example, if the shipowner or charterer provides an unseaworthy vessel a claim by the other interests could be raised.

Lien and adjustment: The general average claims are enforceable among the parties to the marine venture that are secured by a maritime lien.

8.4   York-Antwerp Rules

The York-Antwerp Rules are the result of international conferences, which sought to produce uniformity of practice and to provide a reliable code of behavior. They were in practice generally incorporated into charter parties and bills of lading.

The rules comprise of lettered and numbered rules. The rules of interpretation state in their first paragraph:

"In the adjustment of general average, the following lettered and numbered rules shall apply to the exclusion of any law and practice inconsistent therewith."

The reference to a system of lettered and numbered rules is explained by the desirability of setting forth a series of general principles, which are embodied in the lettered rules, followed by a number of propositions (in rather greater detail), which deal with specific situations. Prior to the existence of the York-Antwerp Rules, the practices of different countries were at variance. The relationship between the lettered and numbered rules is regulated by the second paragraph of the "Rules of Interpretation," which reads:

"Except as provided by the numbered rules, general average shall be adjusted according to the lettered rules."

8.5 Process of Adjustment

Losses admissible in general average are assessed and apportioned over the net arrived-upon values of the property saved plus the value of the sacrificed property that has been admitted in general average. That is, the property sacrificed makes its contribution to the general average losses, in the same way as the property that is saved.

The loss admitted in general average for the account of each of the parties to the venture is compared with the contribution due from him or her, and the parties arrive at a balance either to be paid or to be received. This is the process of general average "adjustment."

A simple example of the calculation as below:

A ship X is carrying cargos for   A valued   U.S. $ 100,000

B valued   U.S.$ 150,000

C valued   U.S.$ 50,000

Ship and equipment valued	U.S.$ 200,000

Total value at risk	U.S.$ 500,000

The ship encountered heavy weather and voluntarily sacrificed the cargo of A which is valued upon arrival U.S.4 100,000. That is , the GA loss is 20% of the total values at risk.

All interest including A should contribute to the loss at 20% of their interest:

A pays	$ 100,000 X 20% = $ 20,000
B pays	$ 150,000X 20% = $ 30,000
C pays	$ 50,000X 20%= $ 10,000
Ship pays	$ 200,000X 20%= $ 40,000

Total Contribution	U.S.$ 100,000

Admission in General Average for Loss/Damage to Goods

The essential elements that constitute a general average sacrifice are

- voluntarily made,
- in time of peril,
- for the common safety/ benefit

Such losses could be categorized as either the direct consequence of general average or referred to as "consequential losses or damages."

Example of losses and damages that are the direct consequences of the GA act follow.

8.5.1 Jettison

Jettison refers to the intentional throwing overboard of goods for the common safety of the ship and cargo, either because it is necessary to lighten the ship or because the presence of the goods onboard constitutes a hazard to the common venture.

Examples:

- Cargo jettisoned in order to restore stability to a ship that is in danger of capsizing.
- Cargo jettisoned in order to lighten a stranded ship so that it may be refloated.
- The jettison of goods that are on fire.

8.5.2 Loss and damage caused by efforts to extinguish fire

Fire is a very real and frequent hazard onboard ships. The causes of fire may be due to spontaneous combustion of cargoes, stevedores smoking in the holds, electrical short circuits, and even frying foods in the ship's galley.

Rule III of the York-Antwerp agreement reads:

"Damage done to a ship and cargo, or either of them, by water or otherwise, including damage by beaching or scuttling a burning ship, in extinguishing a fire onboard the ship, shall be made good as general average, except that no compensation shall be made for smoke or heat, however caused."

8.5.3 Loss or damage caused due to extra handling of cargo for the common safety

All cargoes will receive two "handlings" during the course of the contracted voyage, i.e., on loading and discharging.

What is being discussed is really the rough handling or shifting damages sustained in the course of operations undertaken for the common safety. Some examples follow:

- To correct a dangerous list at sea.
- To obtain access to packages that are to be jettisoned for the common safety.
- To obtain access to the origin of a fire in another part of the stowage.
- In the course of a "forced discharge" to barges alongside in order to lighten a stranded ship.

Rule II of the York-Antwerp (YAR) agreement reads: "Damage done to a ship and cargo, or either of them, by or in consequence of a sacrifice made for the common safety, and by water that goes down a ship's hatches opened or other opening made for the purpose of making a jettison for the common safety, shall be made good as general average."

Rule VIII reads: "When a ship is ashore, and cargo and ship's fuel and stores or any of them are discharged as a general average act, the extra cost of lightening, lighter hire, and reshipping (if incurred), and the loss or damage sustained thereby, shall be admitted as general average."

8.5.4 Consequential losses and damages

These are losses or damages caused in discharging, handling, storing, reloading, and stowing cargo.

These operations may be undertaken for the common safety, for the purpose of effecting essential repairs to the ship, or for purposes that have no connection with general average.

Rule XII of York Antwer Rules (YAR) reads: "Damage to or loss of cargo, fuel, or stores caused in the act of handling, discharging storing, reloading, and stowing shall be made good as general average, when and only when the cost of those measures respectively is admitted as general average."

In practice, loss or damage to cargo that occurs as a direct or foreseeable consequence of its discharge at a port of refuge where facilities are inadequate is admitted in general average.

The following are instances of damages allowed in practice as general average:

- Damage to cargo through the leakage of rainwater through the roof of a warehouse
- Damage to cargo through exposure to weather on account of insufficiency of storage under cover
- Pilferage, insofar as petty thieving would be more or less inevitable at the port or place where the cargo has been landed

8.6 Loss on Sale to Raise Funds to Pay for General Average Expenditure

It is unlikely that such a case may occur today; however, rule XX(20) of the York-Antwerp Rules retains that effect and states:

"The necessary cost of obtaining the funds required by means of a bottomry bond or otherwise, or the loss sustained by owners of goods sold for the purpose, shall be allowed in general average."

8.7 Valuation of the Contributing Interests

The two essential parts in every general average adjustment are the number of the sacrifices and expenditures on one hand and the ascertainment of the value of the property that will contribute to those allowances on the other.

All property that is at risk at the time of the general average act will contribute, but its value for contribution will be based upon its arrived value at its destination.

This principle is written into the York Antwer Rules (YAR) by rule G, which states the following:

"General average shall be adjusted as regards both loss and contribution upon the basis of values at the time and place when and where the venture ends."

8.8 Security for Claims in GA

Under the laws of most maritime nations, a shipowner has a right to hold the cargo at destination until its owner has paid his or her contribution in general average or the net balance due under the adjustment.

However, with the sophistication of maritime commerce, it has become usual to entrust these calculations to an independent person, who is known as an adjuster of average, and the shipowner's right to hold cargo was met by the owner of the cargo providing some alternative security, either in the form of a deposit on account of this ultimate contribution or a form of undertaking.

The customary document by which the receiver of cargo undertakes to perform this obligation is called an "average bond." In addition to the average bond, the shipowner may, and usually does, require additional security, which may take the form of any one of the following:

- A cash deposit
- A guarantee from the underwriters of the goods
- A bank guarantee

When a receiver of cargo signs an average bond, he or she undertakes to furnish the average adjuster with particulars of the value of the goods received. He or she then returns the forms to the average adjuster or the ship's agent together with a copy of the commercial invoice to evidence the sound value of the goods. If the goods arrive subject to loss or damage, they will need to be surveyed. In this event, he or she should retain a valuation form until after the survey has taken place, so that he or she can enter the particulars of the loss or damage before returning the form.

8.8.1 Underwriter's Guarantee

There is a standard form for an underwriter's guarantee issued by the Corporation of Lloyd's, which "guarantees the due payment to the owners of any contribution or general average and/or salvage and/or other charges that may be properly chargeable against the goods. It will be observed that the guarantee is unlimited in time or in amount."

8.8.2 Bank Guarantee

A bank guarantee may occur either where the goods are uninsured or when the standing of the insurers is doubtful. A bank guarantee will be limited in terms of the amount guaranteed. Consequently, in deciding whether or not to accept a bank guarantee, a shipowner will need to have calculated the estimated quantum of the general average and the approximate total values for contribution, in order to assess the amount for which the guarantee is to be given.

There is no standard form of verbiage for a bank guarantee. If a text is submitted by a shipowner or an adjuster, it is likely to be based on the wording employed in an underwriter's guarantee.

8.8.3 Deposit

In the event of cargo being uninsured, or being insured with a company of doubtful standing, the shipowner may demand that the receiver of the goods deposit a sum of money as security for the eventual general average contribution. The shipowner will probably rely on his or her average adjuster to provide advice on the quantum of the deposit, and this involves the adjuster making a "thumbnail" adjustment of the probable extent of the general average allowances and the contributory values.

Note

During the writing of this article, a new and updated version of the York-Antwerp Rules for 2016 was issued and approved by the international maritime community.

All working papers and the final text of the YAR 2016 can be found on the CMI website at www.comitemaritime.org.

CHAPTER 9

THE MARINE INSURANCE ACT OF 1906

This section is added to highlight the importance of the oldest law codifying the cases relating to marine insurance and is still considered the optimal reference for the insurance market.

Articles

9.1 **Marine Insurance Defined**

A contract of marine insurance is a contract whereby the insurer undertakes to indemnify the assured, in a manner and to an extent thereby agreed, against marine losses (the losses incident to marine adventure).

Note

The contract is embodied by a form called the "policy." The party who undertakes to indemnify the other is called the "insurer" or "underwriter." The party to be indemnified is called the "insured."

The consideration that the insurer receives for his or her undertaking is called the "premium." The term "loss" includes damage or detriment as well as the actual loss of the property.

The term "risk" is used in different senses. Sometimes it is used to denote the perils themselves to which insurable property may be exposed, as when sea risks are contracted with land risks, or when goods are insured against "all risks."

Marine insurance in legal theory is essentially a contract of indemnity. The extent and amount of indemnity are matters of agreement between the parties. But it has often been pointed out that, in practice, marine insurance is not a perfect contract of indemnity. For example, under an unvalued policy on goods, in the ordinary form, and without any special clause, the assured would probably receive an amount less than his or her real loss, while under a valued policy, he or she may receive an amount that either exceeds or falls short of the real loss.

9.2   Mixed Sea and Land Risks

1. A contract of marine insurance may, by its express terms, or by usage of trade, be extended so as to protect the assured against losses on inland waters or on land risks, which may be incidental to any sea voyage.
2. Where a ship in course of building, or the launch of a ship, or any adventure analogous to a marine venture, is covered by a policy in the form of a marine policy, the provisions of this act, insofar as are applicable, shall apply thereto; but, except as by this section provided, nothing in this act shall alter or affect any rule of law applicable to any contract of insurance other than a contract of marine insurance as by this act defined.

Note

The normal insurance now contains the "transit" clause, which covers the goods from the time they leave the shipper's warehouse until they reach the warehouse of the consignee. These mixed sea-and-land risks may be compared, through analogy, with "through bills of lading," which are inventions of modern commerce.

9.3 Marine Adventure and Maritime Perils Defined

There is a marine adventure when the following conditions are met:

a. Any ship, goods, or other movables are exposed to maritime perils. Such property is referred to as "insurable property."
b. The earning or acquisition of freight, passage money, commission, profit, or other pecuniary benefit, or the security for any advances, loan, or disbursements, is endangered by the exposure of insurable property to maritime perils.
c. Any liability to a third party may be incurred by the owner of, or other person interested in or responsible for, insurable property, by reason of maritime perils.

The term "maritime perils" denotes the perils consequent on, or incidental to, the navigation of the sea: perils of the seas, fire, war perils, pirates, rovers, thieves, captures, seizures, restraint/detainments of people, jettisons, barratry, and any other perils, either of the like kind, or that may be designated by the policy.

Note

It is the risk or venture of the assured, not the property exposed to peril, which is the subject of insurance. The ship or goods may be lost. What is really insured is the pecuniary interest of the assured in or in respect to the property exposed to peril.

Insurance is sometimes effected against "all risks," or even against "all risks" by land or water. On the other hand, a policy may be confined to only some of the specified perils. In that case, a so-called warranty is added, excluding particular perils, such as those "warranted free from capture, seizure, and detention, and all the consequences of hostilities."

Regarding "all risks" policies, there are certain necessary limits. The expression does not cover inherent vice or wear and tear. It covers a risk, not a certainty; it is something that happens to the subject matter from without, not the natural behavior of the subject matter, being what it is, in the circumstances under which it is carried. Nor is it a loss that the assured brings about by his or her own actions, for then the assured has not merely exposed the goods to the chance of injury, but the assured has injured them himself or herself. The description *all risks* does not alter the general law; only risks are covered that it is lawful to cover, and the onus of proof remains where it would have been on a policy against ordinary sea perils.

9.4 Insurable Interest

Regarding the avoidance of wagering and gaming contracts, the following apply:

1) Every contract of marine insurance by way of gaming or wagering is void.
2) A contract of marine insurance is deemed to be a gaming or wagering contract:
   a) Where the assured has not an insurable interest as defined by this act, and the contract is entered into with no expectation of acquiring such an interest, or
   b) Where the policy is made "interest or no interest" or without further proof of interest than the policy itself

or without benefit of salvage to the insurer or to any other like term,

provided that, where there is no possibility of salvage, a policy may be in effect without benefit of salvage to the insurer.

Note

A policy "without interest" is not necessarily a wager policy. For example, when the assured *bona fide* expects to have an interest, but the expectation is not realized, the policy is not a wager policy. The assured cannot recover on the policy, but he or she may be entitled to a return of the premium.

9.5   Insurable Interest Defined

Subject to the provisions of this act, every person has an insurable interest who is interested in a marine venture:

In particular, a person is interested in a marine venture where he or she stands in any legal or equitable relation to the venture or to any insurable property at risk in consequence of which he or she may benefit by the safety or due arrival of insurable property or may be prejudiced by its loss or by damage thereto or the detention thereof or may incur liability in respect thereof.

Note

Three questions, often confused, must be kept distinct: 1. Has the assured an insurable interest? 2. Is the subject matter, in respect to which the assured's interest arises, sufficiently described in the policy? 3. What is the quantum of this interest?

The definition of *insurable interest* has been continuously expanding, and dicta in some of the older cases, which would tend to narrow it, must be accepted with caution. The essence of interest is a) that there should be a physical object exposed to sea perils; and b) that the assured should stand in some relationship, recognized by law, to that object, in consequence of which he or she either benefits by its preservation or is prejudiced by its loss or by mishap to it.

The general rule is clear: that to constitute interest insurable against a peril, there must be an interest such that the peril would, by its proximate effect, cause damage to the assured.

Any interest that is dependent on the safety of the thing exposed to (the risks insured against) may be insured. Still, it must in all cases at the time of the loss be an interest legal or equitable, and not merely an expectation, however probable.

9.6 When Interest Must Attach

1. The assured must be interested in the subject matter insured at the time of the loss, though he or she need not be interested when the insurance is effected.

Provided that, where the subject matter is insured, "lost or not lost," the assured may recover, although he or she may not have acquired this interest until after the loss unless, at the time of effecting the contract of insurance, the assured was aware of the loss, and the insurer was not.

2. Where the assured has no interest at time of the loss, he or she cannot acquire interest by any act or election after becoming aware of the loss.

Note

It is a difficult question to determine the exact moment when, under a contract of sale, the risk passes from seller to buyer. The risk passes when the property passes, but under the terms of the contract, they may pass at different times. When goods are insured by the buyer, the question is whether (on the true construction of the contract), the risk has passed to him or her at the time when the loss occurs.

9.7   Defeasible and Contingent Interest

(1) A defeasible interest is insurable as a contingent interest.

(2) In particular, where the buyer of goods has insured them, he or she has an insurable interest, notwithstanding that he or she might, by election, have rejected the goods, or have treated them as at the seller's risk, by reason of the latter's delay in making delivery or otherwise.

Note

Regarding contingent interests, the main difficulty is to determine not whether there is an interest but whether the interest has attached at the time of the loss.

When captors of a ship insured it, the prize court afterward restored the ship to its owners, and it was held that the premium was not returnable, for the risk had attached. The interest in this case may be regarded either as defeasible or contingent.

Suppose Person "A" buys goods by sample, to be shipped from abroad, and insures them. Goods that are inferior to sample are shipped and are then partially sea-damaged on the voyage. "A" may accept the goods and claim on the policy. If "A" rejects the goods, presumably he or she could not claim on the policy; but could "A" assign the policy to the seller, and then reject the goods? Presumably, "A" could not, but various complications may be suggested, which still await decision.

9.8 Partial Interest

A partial interest of any nature is insurable.

Note

An undivided interest in a parcel of goods shipped on a free on board (FOB) basis is insurable. So, too, a shareholder may insure his or her interest in the adventure of a company engaged in laying a submarine cable.

The Lloyd's policy is expressed to ensure for the benefit of all to whom the subject matter pertains "in part or in all," but these general words must be limited by the circumstances of the particular insurance.

9.9 Reinsurance

1. The insurer under a contract of marine insurance has an insurable interest in his or her risk, and may reinsure in respect to it.
2. Unless the policy otherwise provides, the original assured has no right or interest in respect to such reinsurance.

Note

Reinsurance is an insurance effected by an insurer to cover wholly or in part the risk he or she has undertaken, and it must be distinguished from "double insurance," which is a second insurance effected by or on behalf of an assured on a risk already covered.

Reinsurance treaties: The Marine Insurance Act of 1906 does not deal with treaties of reinsurance. A treaty of reinsurance is a contract whereby the reinsurer agrees to reinsure the whole or a portion of a specified class or classes of risk to be underwritten by the reassured (original insurer).

The usual form of reinsurance policy runs as being reinsurance subject to all clauses and conditions of the original policy or policies, and to pay as may be paid thereon and then follow the exceptions, if any.

9.10 Bottomry

The lender of money on bottomry or respondentia has an insurable interest in respect to the loan.

Note

By the law of the sea, the master may, in case of necessity, and under certain restrictions, raise money on the security of the ship, freight, and cargo. The conditions of a loan on bottomry or respondentia is that the money is not repayable if the ship or cargo does not arrive. Consequently, it is the lender who must insure.

This section is now of no practical importance, for the practice of lending money on bottomry or respondentia is obsolete.

9.11 Masters' and Seamen's Wages

The master or any member of the crew of a ship has an insurable interest in respect to his or her wages.

Note

The law as to the insurability of seamen's wages was doubtful. The master of a ship could always insure his or her wages, but formerly (at any rate) a seaman under the rank of a master could not. "Wages of seamen," according to the judges in an old case, are by their nature insurable, though universally prohibited to be insured on principles of policy. But when this was laid down, the doctrine that "freight was the mother of wages" prevailed, and if freight was not earned, the seaman was not entitled to wages.

The doctrine was abandoned by the Merchant Shipping Act of 1854, and it was provided that the right to wages should not be dependent on the earning of freight.

9.12 Advance Freight

In the case of advance freight, the person advancing the freight has an insurable interest, insofar as such freight is not repayable in case of loss.

Note

By English law, advance freight as such is not repayable in case of loss. The shipowner therefore does not have an insurable interest in it, but the person advancing it has. But by special contract, it may be repayable, and then the positions are reversed.

Though advanced freight may be repayable in case of loss, the shipowner may be liable in damages to the cargo owner if the loss is occasioned by his or her negligence or fault, and in estimating the damages, the amount advanced for freight must be taken into account.

By the law of most foreign countries, advance freight is repayable in case of loss.

9.13 Charges of Insurance

The assured has an insurable interest in the charges of any insurance that he or she may bring into effect.

Note

Ordinarily, the charges of insurance consist of the premium and the brokerage if paid by the assured. In practice, the broker's commission is paid by the insurer.

9.14 Quantum of Interest

(1) Where the subject matter is mortgaged, the mortgagor has an insurable interest in the full value thereof, and the mortgagee has an insurable interest in respect to any sum due or to become due under the mortgage.

(2) A mortgagee, consignee, or other person having an interest in the subject matter insured may insure on behalf and for the benefit of other persons interested as well as for his or her own benefit.

(3) The owner of insurable property has an insurable interest in respect to the full value thereof, notwithstanding that some third person may have agreed, or be liable, to indemnify him or her in case of loss.

Note

A person with a limited interest may insure either for himself or herself and to cover his or her own interest only, or the person may insure so as to cover not merely his or her own limited interest, but the interest of all others who are interested in the property. Where two or more persons insure the same subject matter so as to exceed the insurable value, the equities are worked out by the principle of subrogation, and contribution between insurers.

9.15 Assignment of Interest

Where the assured assigns or otherwise parts with his or her interest in the subject matter insured, the assured does not thereby transfer to the assignee his or her rights under the contract of insurance, unless there be an express or implied agreement with the assignee to that effect.

But the provisions of this section do not effect a transmission of interest by operation of law.

Note

Where the subject matter of the insurance is sold during the running of the policy, no interest under the policy passes unless it is made part of the contract of purchase and sale, so that it would be considered in a court of equity as assigned.

Where there is such an agreement, it may be given effective to either by an assignment of the policy, or by the assignor holding the policy as trustee for the assignee.

Insurable Value
9.16 Measure of Insurable Value

Subject to any express provision or valuation in the policy, the insurable value of the subject matter insured must be ascertained as follows:

(1) In insurance on ship, the insurable value at the commencement of the risk of the ship, including its outfit, provisions, and stores for the officers and crew, money advanced for seamen's wages, and other disbursements (if any) incurred to make the ship fit for the voyage or venture contemplated by the policy, plus the charges of insurance upon the whole.

The insurable value, in the case of a steamship, includes also the machinery, boilers, and engine stores if owned by the assured, and, in the case of a ship engaged in a special trade, the ordinary fittings requisite for that trade.

(2) In insurance on freight, whether paid in advance or otherwise, the insurable value is the gross amount of the freight at the risk of the assured, plus the charges of insurance.

(3) In insurance on goods or merchandise, the insurable value is the prime cost of the property insured, plus the expenses of and incidental to shipping and the charges of insurance upon the whole.

(4) In insurance on any other subject matter, the insurable value is the amount at risk of the assured when the policy attaches, plus the charges of insurance.

Note

Though marine insurance is universally admitted to be a contract of indemnity, there are two opposing theories as to what is the nature of the indemnity to be aimed at. According to some, the assured ought to be put in the same position as if he or she had not undertaken the venture. According to others, he or she ought to be put in the same position as if the venture had been carried to a successful closure. English law steers a halting course between these two theories, but with a strong leaning toward the former.

According to modern practice, unvalued policies are very rare, being practically confined to goods and in a few instances to freight payable on arrival. Other interests are almost invariably insured by valued policies. When the amount to be insured on goods cannot be fixed until the receipt of what are known as "closing particulars." Provision is usually made that, in the event of loss before declaration, the declaration shall be on the basis of invoice cost and charges, plus a certain agreed percentage for anticipated profits.

A voyage policy on goods is an insurance of the venture, as well as an insurance on the goods themselves.

9.17 Disclosure and Representation
Insurance is *uberrimae fidei*
A contract of marine insurance is a contract based upon the utmost good faith, and, if the utmost good faith be not observed by either party, the contract may be voided by the other party.

Note

Insurance is a contract based on utmost good faith, and the obligation is binding upon both parties alike, though necessarily the question usually arises with reference to the conduct of the assured. "Good faith" forbids either party, by concealing what he or she privately knows, to draw the other into a bargain from ignorance of that fact, and from believing the contrary.

9.18 Disclosure by Assured

(1) Subject to the provisions of this act, the assured must disclose to the insurer, before the contract is concluded, every

material circumstance that is known to the assured, and the assured is deemed to know every circumstance that, in the ordinary course of business, ought to be known by him or her. If the assured fails to make such disclosure, the insurer may avoid the contract.

(2) Every circumstance is material, which would influence the judgment of a prudent insurer in fixing the premium or determining whether he or she will take the risk.

(3) In the absence of inquiry, the following circumstances need not be disclosed:

(a) Any circumstance that diminishes the risk

(b) Any circumstance that is known or presumed to be known to the insurer; the insurer is presumed to know matters of common notoriety or knowledge and matters that an insurer in the ordinary course of his or her business, as such, ought to know

(c) Any circumstance as to which information is waived by the insurer

(d) Any circumstance that it is superfluous to disclose by reason of any express or implied warranty

(4) Whether any particular circumstance, which is not disclosed, be material or not is, in such case, a question of fact.

(5) The term "circumstance" includes any communication made to or information received by the assured.

Note

Nondisclosure by the assured is sometimes referred to as "concealment," but the expression "nondisclosure" is preferable. The duty of the assured to disclose material facts is a positive, not a negative, duty. Mere silence, and even innocent silence, as to material fact entitles the insurer to avoid the contract. The duty of disclosure is confined to questions of fact"; "a question of opinion is not a material circumstance within the act."

The assured is deemed to know every circumstance that, in the ordinary course of business, ought to be known by him or her. Consequently, where the assured effects an insurance policy himself or herself, knowledge of a material fact by the agent of the assured will be imputed to the assured.

It is to be observed that the test as to what is a material circumstance is that it must be one that would influence a prudent insurer in fixing the premium or determining whether he or she will take the risk.

9.19 Disclosure by Agent Effecting Insurance

Subject to the provisions of the preceding section as to circumstances that need not be disclosed where an insurance is effected for the assured by an agent, the agent must disclose to the insurer:

(a) Every material circumstance that is known to the agent, and an agent to insure is deemed to know every circumstance that, in the ordinary course of business, ought to be known by, or to have been communicated to, him or her; and

(b) Every material circumstance that the assured is bound to disclose, unless it come to his or her knowledge too late to communicate it to the agent.

Note

The knowledge of an agent to insure, who does not effect the particular insurance, is immaterial, but if an agent to insure employs a subagent, all material facts known to the agent must be communicated to the subagent.

If, before the contract is made, the assured hears of a loss but has not time to communicate with his or her agent, the

THE MARINE INSURANCE HANDBOOK

contract would stand. The assured must use due diligence to communicate with the agent.

9.20   Representations Pending Negotiation of Contract

(1) Every material representation made by the assured or the assured's agent to the insurer during the negotiations for the contract, and before the contract is concluded, must be true. If they be untrue, the insurer may avoid the contract.

(2) A representation is material that would influence the judgment of a prudent insurer in fixing the premium or determining whether he or she will take the risk.

(3) A representation may be either a representation as to matter of fact, or as to a matter of expectation or belief.

(4) A representation as to a matter of fact is true if it be substantially correct; that is to say, if the difference between what is represented and what is actually correct would not be considered material by a prudent insurer.

(5) A representation as to a matter of expectation or belief is true if it be made in good faith.

(6) A representation may be withdrawn or corrected before the contract is concluded.

(7) Whether a particular representation be material or not is, in each case, a question of fact.

Note

A relative English court ruling stated that "the assured is not bound to tell the insurer what the law is. He is bound to tell him, not every fact, but every material fact. His other obligation is this, that if he is asked a question, whether a material fact or not, by the underwriters, though it may not be a material fact, it will vitiate the policy."

It is sufficient if a representation to expectation or belief is made in good faith. The assured must have reasonable ground for his or her belief.

Representations may be made orally or in writing. A representation expressed in, or implied from the terms of the policy itself, constitutes a warranty. The policy is the final expression of the contract. A representation differs from a warranty in this: a warranty must be exactly complied with, while it is sufficient if a representation is substantially correct.

The assured or his or her agent is not bound to give an opinion to the insurer on any matter relating to the venture. The assured is bound to disclose facts. For example, the assured may think that war between two states is imminent; but unless the assured has special information, he or she may leave the insurer to form the insurer's own judgment on the matter.

9.21   When Contract is Deemed to Be Concluded

A contract of marine insurance is deemed to be concluded when the proposal of the assured is accepted by the insurer, whether the policy be then issued or not; and for the purpose of showing when the proposal was accepted, reference may be made to the slip or covering note or another customary memorandum of the contract.

Note

In effecting marine insurance, the matter is considered merely as negotiation until the slip is initialed, but when that is done, the contract is considered to be concluded. It was proved to be the duty of underwriters to issue a stamped policy in accordance with the slip, notwithstanding anything that might happen after the initialing of the slip.

THE MARINE INSURANCE HANDBOOK

The Policy
9.22 Contract Must Be Embodied in Policy

Subject to the provisions of any statute, a contract of marine insurance is inadmissible in evidence unless it is embodied in a marine policy in accordance with this act. The policy may be executed and issued either at the time when the contract is concluded or afterward.

Note

When a policy has been duly issued, reference may be made to the "slip" for the purpose of showing when the contract was concluded or for the purpose of rectifying or avoiding the policy.

9.23 What the Policy Must Specify

A marine policy must specify the name of the assured, or of some person who brings into effect the insurance on his or her behalf.

Note

The Marine Insurance Act of 1788, now repealed in regard to marine insurance, was construed as merely prohibiting insurances in blank or to a bearer and is therefore sufficiently reproduced by this section.

Where different interests are concerned, it is common practice for the broker to enter into the policy in his or her own name but on behalf of and to protect the interest of different constituents.

9.24 Signature of Insurer

1) A marine policy must be signed by or on behalf of the insurer, provided that in case of corporation, the

corporate seal may be sufficient, but nothing in this section shall be construed as requiring the subscription of a corporation to be under seal.

2) Where a policy is substituted by or on behalf of two or more insurers, each subscription, unless the contrary be expressed, constitutes a distinct contract with the assured.

Note

A marine policy is incomplete and revocable until delivery to, or for the benefit of, the person entitled to hold it. In the case of an insurance company's policy, delivery is presumed on very slight evidence. In the case of Lloyd's policies, the broker formerly obtained the underwriters' signatures directly. They are now affixed by the Lloyd's Policy Signing Office.

9.25 Voyage and Time Policies

Where the contract is to insure the subject matter "at and from" or from one place to another or others, the policy is called a "voyage policy," and where the contract is to insure the subject matter for a definite period of time, the policy is called a "time policy." A contract for both voyage and time may be included in the same policy.

Note

A ship may be insured "from London to Hong Kong for six months," or "from London to New York, and thirty days after arrival."

The word "definite" means that the period must be specified. It is sufficiently specified if it denotes a stated period, even though that period is determinable on notice and even

THE MARINE INSURANCE HANDBOOK

though the insurance will be renewed or continued automatically at the end of the period unless determined.

Time policies sometimes give rise to difficult questions in which the cause of loss comes into operation before the policy expires, but the actual loss occurs after it expires.

9.26 Designation of the Subject Matter

The subject matter insured must be designated in a marine policy with reasonable certainty.

The nature and extent of the interest of the assured in the subject matter insured need not be specified in the policy.

Where the policy designates the subject matter in general terms, it shall be construed to apply to the interest intended by the assured to be covered.

In the application of this section, regard shall be given to any usage regulating the designation of the subject matter insured.

Note

The quantum of the assured's interest need not be specified in the policy. Thus, it is not necessary to specify whether the assured insures for himself or herself or as trustee for another, as full owner, or as mortgagor or mortgagee.

The subject matter is usually very briefly described as being "on ship," "on goods," and "on freight," but the description must not be misleading. Thus, a policy on *piece goods* will not cover a loss on hats, so, too a policy "on freight" will not cover passage money.

127

Subsection 3 is intended to protect the assured against technical objections to the description of the interest insured, and to give effect to the real intention of the contract where the wording was ambiguous.

9.27   Valued Policy

1. A policy may be either valued or unvalued.
2. A valued policy is a policy that specifies the agreed value of the subject matter insured.
3. Subject to the provisions of this act, and in the absence of fraud, the value fixed by the policy is, as between the insurer and assured, conclusive of the insurable value of the subject intended to be insured, whether the loss be total or partial.
4. Unless the policy otherwise provided, the value fixed by the policy is not conclusive for the purpose of determining whether there has been a constructive total loss.

Note

An unvalued policy is sometimes spoken of as an "open policy," but as that term is applied in business language to a floating policy, the act uniformly uses the term "unvalued policy." The effect of the valuation was merely to fix the insurable value of the goods or other subject matter insured. In an open policy, the compensation must be ascertained by evidence; in a valued policy, the agreed total value is conclusive.

The valuation is conclusive for all purposes relating to the insurable value of the subject matter insured by a given policy.

Notwithstanding the valuation, the interest of the assured may be disproved, or short interest may be shown, or it may

THE MARINE INSURANCE HANDBOOK

be shown that the whole or part of the subject matter insured was not at risk.

Overvaluation made in good faith is not grounds for avoiding the policy or reducing the amount payable under it, but gross overvaluation, if not disclosed, is evidence of fraud. Apart from fraud, gross overinsurance, even by collateral *honor* policies, unless disclosed, will enable the insurer to avoid the contract.

9.28   Unvalued Policy

An unvalued policy is a policy that does not specify the value of the subject matter insured, but, subject to the limit of the sum insured, leaves the insurable value to be subsequently ascertained.

Note

Unvalued policies are found only rarely.

9.29   Floating Policy by Ship or Ships

1. A floating policy is a policy that describes the insurance in general terms and leaves the name of the ship or ships and other particulars to be defined by subsequent declaration.
2. The subsequent declaration or declarations may be made by endorsement on the policy or in other customary manner.
3. Unless the policy otherwise provides, the declarations must be made in the order of dispatch or shipment. They must, in the case of goods, comprise all consignments within the terms of the policy, and the value of the goods or other property must be honestly stated, but an omission or erroneous declaration may be rectified even after

the loss or arrival, provided the omission or declaration was made in good faith.

4. Unless the policy otherwise provides, where a declaration of value is not made until after notice of loss or arrival, the policy must be treated as an unvalued policy as regards the subject matter of that declaration.

Note

The legality of the practice of creating floating policies was affirmed in England in 1794.

Floating policies are now commonly effected "to follow and succeed"; thus, the prior policy must be exhausted before the next policy is declared on.

9.30　　Construction of Terms in Policy

1. A policy may be in the form in the first schedule of this act.
2. Subject to the provisions of this act, and unless the context of the policy otherwise requires, the terms and expressions mentioned in the first schedule of this act shall be construed as having the scope and meaning in that schedule assigned by them.

Note

The rules in the schedule record the interpretation that has been put on the more important terms and expressions in the Lloyd's policy. This may assist the parties to see the scope and effect of the ordinary printed contract, and to add or alter its terms to meet their requirements

9.31 Premium to be Arranged

1. Where an insurance is effected at a premium to be arranged, and no arrangement is made, a reasonable premium is payable.
2. Where an insurance is effected on the terms that an additional premium is to be arranged in a given event, and that event happens but no arrangement is made, then a reasonable additional premium is payable.

Note

Policies are often effected on the terms that a deviation or a change of voyage or an error in description or a breach of a warranty shall be "held covered at a premium to be arranged."

What constitutes a reasonable premium, or additional premium, is a question of fact.

9.32 Double Insurance

1. Where two or more policies are effected by or on behalf of the assured on the same venture and interest or any part thereof, and the sums insured exceed the indemnity allowed by this act, the assured is said to be overinsured by double insurance.
2. Where the assured is overinsured by double insurance:
   a. The assured, unless the policy otherwise provides, may claim payment from the insurers in such order as he or she may think fit, provided that he or she is not entitled to receive any sum in excess of the indemnity allowed by this act.

b. Where the policy under which the assured claims is a valued policy, the assured must give credit as against the valuation, for any sum received by him or her under any other policy without regard to the actual value of the subject matter insured.

c. Where the policy under which the assured claims is an unvalued policy, he or she must give credit, as against the full insurable value, for any sum received by him or her under any other policy.

d. Where the assured receives any sum in excess of the indemnity allowed by this act, the assured is deemed to hold such sums in trust for the insurers, according to their right of contribution among themselves.

Note

Insurance is a contract of indemnity, and the assured is entitled to indemnity but not to a gambling profit. Similarly, the insurer must not make a profit where he or she runs no risk. The English rule that the same subject matter may be differently valued in different policies, while the valuation in a policy is conclusive for the purposes of that policy, gives rise to curious anomalies in working out the rules of double insurance under valued policies.

Different assured: This question arises when the same subject matter is fully insured by persons who have different interests in it (for instance, mortgagor and mortgagee, or bailor and bailee). The case was discussed in a fire policy in which both the merchant and the wharfinger insured the same goods against fire. The goods were destroyed by fire, and it was held that the loss must be wholly borne by the wharfinger's insurers, as the wharfinger was liable to the merchant.

In the case of marine policy, contribution only applies where it is an insurance by the same person having the same rights, and it does not apply where different persons insure in regard to different rights.

Warranties and so Forth
9.33 Nature of warranty

1. A warranty in the following sections relating to warranties, means a promissory warranty, which is a warranty where the assured undertakes that some particular thing shall or shall not be done, or that some condition shall be fulfilled, or whereby he or she affirms or negates the existence of a particular state of facts.
2. A warranty may be expressed or implied.
3. A warranty, as above defined, is a condition that must be exactly complied with, whether it be material to the risk or not. If it be not so complied with, then subject to any express provision in the policy, the insurer is discharged from liability as from the date of the breach of warranty but without prejudice to any liability incurred by him or her before that date.

Note

The use of the term "warranty" as signifying a condition precedent is inveterate in marine insurance, but it is unfortunate, because in other branches of the law of contract, the term has a different meaning. For example, in relation to the law of sale of goods, it signifies a collateral stipulation, the breach of which gives rise merely to a claim for damages and not to a right to avoid the contract.

A warranty in marine insurance is used to denote a condition to be fulfilled by the assured and to be a limitation on or an exception from the general words of the policy. In the case of a promissory warranty, for example, when a ship sets sail on or before a particular date, the insurer may avoid the contract if the warranty is not exactly complied with. But in the case of the warranty "free from capture and seizure," the assured does not undertake that the ship or cargo shall not be captured. There is merely a stipulation that the policy shall not apply to such a loss.

A breach of warranty does not necessarily make the policy void. A void contract cannot be ratified, but a breach of warranty may be waived. A breach of warranty in insurance law appears to stand on the same footing as the breach of a condition in any other branch of the law of contract. When a breach of warranty is proved, the insurer is discharged from further liability, unless the assured proved that the breach has been waived. A special clause is often inserted, holding the assured covered in the event of breach of warranty at a premium to be arranged.

The onus of proving a breach of warranty lies on the insurer.

9.34   When Breach of Warranty is Excused

1. Noncompliance with a warranty is excused when, by reason of a change of circumstances, the warranty ceases to be applicable to the circumstances of the contract, or when compliance with the warranty is rendered unlawful by any subsequent law.
2. Where a warranty is broken, the assured cannot avail himself or herself of the defense that the breach has been remedied and the warranty complied with before loss.
3. A breach of warranty may be waived by the insurer.

Note

The reported cases assume that there is no distinction between the effect of an express and an implied warranty. But an implied warranty may be negated by the terms of the policy. For example, the implied warranty of seaworthiness in a voyage policy may be made negative by the "unseaworthiness and unfitness exclusion clause."

To examine a change of circumstances excusing compliance with a warranty, make the supposition that a ship is warranted to sail on or before a particular day, but owing to the outbreak of war, it has to wait for a convoy. In that case, the policy would probably never attach. On the other hand, a ship may be warranted to sail with a convoy, but if peace is made, the warranty becomes inapplicable.

9.35   Express Warranty

1. An express warranty may be expressed in any form of words that the intention to warrant is to be inferred.
2. An express warranty must be included in, or written upon, the policy, or must be contained in some document incorporated by reference into the policy.
3. An express warranty does not exclude an implied warranty, unless it be inconsistent therewith.

Note

The following are instances of express warranties, which have been the subject of judicial interpretation:

"Warranted sailing on or after March 1…"

"Warranted the master of the insured vessel shall be…"

"Warranted subject to a satisfactory survey by approved surveyors…"

9.36 Warranty of Neutrality

1. Where insurable property, whether a ship or goods, is expressly warranted neutral, there is an implied condition that the property shall have a neutral character at the commencement of the risk, and that, so far as the assured can control the matter, its neutral character shall be preserved during the risk.
2. Where a ship is expressly warranted neutral, there is also an implied condition that, so far as the assured can control the matter, it shall be properly documented; thus, its papers shall not be falsified, suppressed, or simulated papers. If any loss occurs through breach of this condition, the insurer may avoid the contract.

Note

The implied conditions may be negated or varied by terms of the particular express warranty.

The conditions of maritime commerce and war have altered so much that it would be misleading to attempt to deduce any rule from the numerous decisions at the beginning of the last century as to the effect of the warranty to sail with convoy.

9.37 No Implied Warranty of Nationality

There is no implied warranty as to nationality of a ship or that its nationality shall not be changed during the risk.

Note

Suppose the assured changes the nationality of the ship, and thereby, it exposes the ship to risk of hostile capture. Possibly, in that case, the loss would be attributed to the act of the assured rather than to capture.

9.38 Warranty of Good Safety

Where the subject matter insured is warranted "well" or "in good safety" on a particular day, it is sufficient if it be safe at any time during that day.

Note

Section 18 of this act is relative in respect to disclosure of facts known to the assured before the contract is concluded.

9.39 Warranty of Seaworthiness of Ship

1. In a voyage policy, there is an implied warranty that at the commencement of the voyage, the ship shall be seaworthy for the purpose of the particular venture insured.
2. Where the policy attaches while the ship in port, there is also an implied warranty that it shall, at the commencement of the risk, be reasonably fit to encounter the ordinary perils of the port.
3. Where the policy relates to a voyage that is performed in different stages, during which the ship requires different kinds of, or further, preparation or equipment, there is an implied warranty that at the commencement of each stage, the ship is seaworthy in respect to such preparation or equipment for the purposes of that stage.
4. A ship is deemed to be seaworthy when it is reasonably fit in all respects to encounter perils of the seas of the venture insured.
5. In a time policy, there is no implied warranty that the ship be seaworthy at any stage of the venture, but where,

with the privity of the assured, the ship is sent to sea in an unseaworthy state, the insurer is not liable for any loss attributable to unseaworthiness.

Note

The implied warranty (that the ship is seaworthy) attaches to every voyage policy, whether on ship, freight, cargo, profits, commission, or other interest. The warranty applies only to the commencement of the voyage, or, as the case may be, of each distinct stage of the voyage. A ship is seaworthy when it is in fit state, "as to repair, equipment, and crew, and in all other respects, to encounter the ordinary perils of the voyage insured at the time of sailing upon it."

The state of seaworthiness is a relative and not an absolute one. It must be determined with reference to the particular voyage and venture in contemplation.

The burden of proving unseaworthiness ordinarily lies on the insurer.

9.40   No Implied Warranty that Goods Are Seaworthy

1. In a policy on goods or other movables, there is no implied warranty that the goods or movables are seaworthy.
2. In a voyage policy on goods or other movables, there is an implied warranty that at the commencement of the voyage, the ship is not only seaworthy as a ship, but also that it is reasonably fit to carry the goods or other movables to the destination denoted in the policy.

Note

Questions of unseaworthiness frequently arise in cases between shippers and shipowners, but such cases must be applied with caution in insurance law. A ship may be seaworthy with consideration between shipowner and insurer on a ship, though unseaworthy with consideration between shipowner and shipper of a particular cargo (such as frozen meat, which requires a special freezing apparatus), but that does not affect the safety of the ship. Again, the warranty regarding goods may apply at a different time from the warranty as to ship, as in the case where goods are shipped at an intermediate port.

In practice, the policy contains an "unseaworthiness and unfitness" clause stating the following: "The underwriters waive any breach of the implied warranties of the seaworthiness of the ship and fitness of the ship to carry the subject matter insured to destination, unless the assured or their employees are privy to such unseaworthiness or unfitness."

9.41   Warranty of Legality

There is an implied warranty that the venture is a lawful one, and that, so far as the assured can control the matter, the venture shall be carried out in a lawful manner.

Note

When a voyage is illegal, an insurance upon such a voyage is invalid. A contract to perform an act that cannot be performed without a violation of the law is void, whether the parties know the law or not.

The term "contraband of war" in a marine policy applies only to goods or merchandise. It does not extend to persons (such as officers of a belligerent power), though carrying them exposes the ship to capture.

If, in a policy on goods, there is a warranty specifying "no contraband," the whole policy may be voided if any part of the goods is contraband.

The Voyage
9.42   Implied Warranty as to Commencement of Risk

1. Where the subject matter is insured by a voyage policy "at and from" or from "a particular place," it is not necessary that the ship should be at that place when the contract is concluded, but there is an implied condition that the venture shall be commenced within a reasonable time, and that if the venture be not so commenced, the insurer may void the contract.

2. The implied condition may be negative by showing that the delay was caused by circumstances known to the insurer before the contract was concluded, or by showing that he or she waived the condition.

Note

"Reasonable time" is a question of fact. Where the assured abandons the venture insured, the contract of marine insurance is determined. The termination of the venture by not commencing the voyage within a reasonable time appears to be distinct from the implied condition that the risk shall not be altered by delay or otherwise.

9.43   Alteration of Port of Departure
Where the place of departure is specified by the policy, and the ship instead of sailing from that place sails from any other place, the risk does not attach.

Note

By usage, an intermediate voyage may be interposed, but the evidence of such a usage would have to be very clear. Suppose a ship is insured from London to New York. If it commences from Southampton or Liverpool, it is a wholly different risk.

THE MARINE INSURANCE HANDBOOK

9.44   Sailing for Different Destination

Where the destination is specified in the policy, and the ship, instead of sailing for that destination, sails for any other destination, the risk does not attach.

Note

For example, consider this hypothetical situation. A policy is taken out on a ship from port "A" port to port "C." It cleared from port "A" to port "D" and was captured. The insurer was not liable, for the policy never attached, because the voyage that commenced was not the one originally insured.

9.45   Change of Voyage

1. Where, after the commencement of the risk, the destination of the ship is voluntarily changed from the destination defined in the policy, there is said to be a change of voyage.
2. Unless the policy otherwise provides, when there is a change of voyage, the insurer is discharged from liability as from the time of change; thus, from the time when the destination to change is manifested, it is immaterial that the ship has not in fact left the course of the voyage defined by the policy when the loss occurs.

Note

Three different states of fact must be distinguished. First, the ship may sail on a voyage not contemplated by the policy. In that case, the risk does not attach. Secondly, a ship may commence the venture insured but afterward may change its destination. There is then a change of voyage. In that case, the risk attaches but is afterward avoided. Thirdly, a ship may proceed from the terminus *a quo* to the terminus *ad quem* but sail there by an unauthorized route. In that case, there is a deviation.

A change of voyage must be voluntary, but very clear evidence of *force majeure* is required in order to continue the insurer's liability when the destination is altered.

In practice, a clause of the policy usually states the following: "Where, after attachment of this insurance, the destination is changed by the assured, it is held covered at a premium and on conditions to be arranged subject to prompt notice being given to the underwriters."

9.46 Deviation

1. Where a ship, without lawful excuse, deviates from the voyage contemplated by the policy, the insurer is discharged from liability as from the time of deviation, and it is immaterial that the ship may have regained its route before any loss occurs.
2. There is a deviation from the voyage contemplated by the policy when the following situations occur:
   (a) Where the course of the voyage is specifically designated by the policy, and that course is departed from, or
   (b) Where the course of the voyage is not specifically designated by the policy, but the usual and customary course is departed from, or
   (c) The intention to deviate is immaterial; there must be a deviation in fact to discharge the insurer from his or her liability under the contract

Note

It is immaterial that the insurer may not be prejudiced by the deviation. Apart from the authority to deviate, a deviation may be waived by the insurer.

In practice, it is usual to include a transit clause in the policy. This provides that the "insurance shall remain in force...during...any deviation."

9.47　Several Ports of Discharge

1. Where several ports of discharge are specified by the policy, the ship may proceed to all or any of them, but in the absence of any usage or sufficient cause to the contrary, it must proceed to them, or to such of them as it travels, in the order designated by the policy. If it does not, there is a deviation.
2. Where the policy references "ports of discharge" within a given area, which are not named, the ship must, in the absence of any usage or sufficient cause to the contrary, proceed to them, or to such of them as the ship visits, in their geographical order. If the ship does not, there is a deviation.

Note

Where the policy specifies the voyage at more than one port, the ship may call on all or any of the places named in the policy; with this reserve only, that if the ship visited more than one place, it must visit them in the order described in the policy.

9.48　Delay in Voyage

In the case of a voyage policy, the venture insured must be prosecuted throughout its course with reasonable dispatch, and, if without lawful excuse it is not so prosecuted, the insurer is discharged from liability from the time when the delay became unreasonable.

Note

Unjustifiable delay in prosecuting the voyage is usually classed under the heading of deviation, but it seems clearer to draw a distinction between time and locality. Reasonable dispatch is a question of fact.

In practice, it is usual to include a transit clause in the policy. This provides that the "insurance shall remain in force...during delay beyond the control of the assured."

9.49   Excuses for Deviation or Delay

1. Deviation or delay in prosecuting the voyage contemplated by the policy is excused:
    a) Where authorized by any special term in the policy, or
    b) Where caused by circumstances beyond the control of the master and his or her employer, or
    c) Where reasonably necessary in order to comply with an express or implied warranty, or
    d) Where reasonably necessary for the safety of the ship or subject matter insured, or
    e) For the purpose of saving human life, or aiding a ship in distress where human life may be in danger, or
    f) Where reasonably necessary for the purpose of obtaining medical or surgical aid for any person onboard the ship, or
    g) Where caused by the barratrous conduct of the master or crew, if barratry be one of the perils insured against
2. When the cause excusing the deviation or delay ceases to operate, the ship must resume its course and prosecute its voyage with reasonable dispatch.

Note

Where a policy contains a "held covered" clause, its scope must be determined in each case by its own particular wording.

Assignment of Policy
9.50   When and How Policy Is Assignable

1. A marine policy is assignable unless it contains terms expressly prohibiting assignment. It may be assigned either before or after loss.
2. Where a marine policy has been assigned to pass the beneficial interest in such a policy, the assignee of the policy is entitled to sue thereon in his or her own name, and the defendant is entitled to make any defense arising out of the contract that he or she would have been entitled to make if the action had been brought in the name of the person by whom or on behalf of whom the policy was effected.
3. A marine policy may be assigned by endorsement thereon or in another customary manner.

Note

Special provisions concerning assignment are set out in clause 22 of the Institute Time Clauses—Hulls.

When a policy is effected by an agent in his or her own name, the person for whose benefit it was effected can always sue on it in his or her own name. A marine policy may be assigned in any way by which an ordinary chosen action may be assigned.

9.51 Assured Who Has No Interest Cannot Assign

When the assured has parted with, or lost interest in, the subject matter insured, and has not, before or at the time of so doing, expressly or implicitly agreed to assign the policy, any subsequent assignment of the policy is inoperative, provided that nothing in this section affects the assignment of a policy after loss.

After loss, the right to indemnity accrues and is fixed, and this right can be assigned. It is everyday practice, where a ship has sustained damage, to sell the injured hull for the benefit of whom it concerns and then sue on the policy. If it can be discerned that the loss is total, the sale is for the benefit of the underwriters, who pay the total loss. If the loss proves only partial, it is for the benefit of the assured.

The Premium
9.52 When the Premium Is Payable

Unless otherwise agreed, the duty of the assured or his or her agent to pay the premium and the duty of the insurer to issue the policy to the assured or his or her agent are concurrent conditions, and the insurer is not bound to issue the policy until payment or tender of the premium.

Note

The term "agreed" includes a binding usage, for usage is binding as being an implied term of the agreement.

Payment, it is to be noted, is not a technical term. It includes a settlement in account when that is an agreed way of doing business.

The broker, in drawing up a policy, is not the insurer's agent or responsible to him or her for any lack of care.

9.53 Policy Effected through Broker

1. Unless otherwise agreed, when a marine policy is effected on behalf of the assured by a broker, the broker is directly responsible to the insurer for the premium, and the insurer is directly responsible to the assured for the amount that may be payable in respect to losses, or in regard to a returnable premium.
2. Unless otherwise agreed, the broker has, as against the assured, a lien upon the policy for the amount of the premium and his or her charges in respect to effecting the policy, and where the broker has dealt with the person who employs him or her as a principal, he or she has also a lien on the policy in respect to any balance on any insurance amount that may be due from such a person, unless when the debt was incurred, the broker had reason to believe that such person was only an agent.

Note

In a case on an insurance company's policy in which, instead of reciting payment of the premium, there was a promise by the assured to pay it, it was held that the ordinary custom applied, and the broker, not the assured, was liable to the insurer for the premium.

It is a well-recognized practice in marine insurance for the broker to treat himself or herself as responsible to the underwriter for the premium; by a fiction he is deemed to have paid the underwriter, and to have borrowed from him the money with which he pays.

In the absence of express authority from his or her principal, a broker cannot cancel a policy, whether it is left in the broker's hands or not. But when a broker who is employed in a foreign country effects a policy in England, he or she has implied authority to cancel the policy if such authority is conferred on him or her by the law of the foreign country.

9.54 Effect of Receipt on Policy

Where a marine policy effected on behalf of the assured by a broker acknowledges the receipt of the premium, such acknowledgment is, in the absence of fraud, conclusive as being between the insurer and the assured but not as between the insurer and broker.

Note

The acknowledgment is not conclusive as being between the insurer and the broker. But, then it is not conclusive as between insurer and assured, where the latter affects the policy directly. However, it is conclusive in favor of an assignee for value without notice.

Loss and Abandonment
9.55 Included and Excluded Losses

1. Subject to the provisions of this act, and unless the policy otherwise provides, the insurer is liable for any loss proximately caused by a peril insured against, but, subject as aforesaid, he or she is not liable for any loss that is not proximately caused by a peril insured against.
2. In particular:
   a. The insurer is not liable for any loss attributable to the willful misconduct of the assured, but, unless the policy otherwise provides, he or she is liable for any loss proximately caused by a peril insured against, even though the loss would not have happened but for the misconduct or negligence of the master or crew;

b. Unless the policy otherwise provides, the insurer on ship or goods is not liable for any loss proximately caused by delay, although the delay be caused by a peril insured against;

c. Unless the policy otherwise provides, the insurer is not liable for ordinary wear and tear; ordinary leakage and breakage, inherent vice, or nature of the subject matter insured, or for any loss proximately caused by rats or vermin, or for any injury to machinery not proximately caused by maritime perils.

Note

Proximate cause rule: No principle of marine insurance law is better established than the rule *causa proxima, non remota*, and *spectator*. It would be infinite for the law to judge the causes of causes and their impulsion one of another; therefore, it contents itself with the immediate cause.

When there are interacting causes of loss, the efficient or *dominating* cause is deemed to be the proximate cause.

Negligence: In the case of negligent or unskillful navigation, it now appears to be settled that the loss is regarded as caused proximately by perils of the seas and only remotely by the negligence or unskillfulness of the master or crew. But when the loss is consequent on the willful act of the assured, that act or default must be regarded as proximately causing the loss.

Where, however, a ship is lost through the barratry of the master, who is a part owner, the innocent co-owners are entitled to recover.

Scuttling: When the insurers allege that a vessel has been scuttled, the matter must be pleaded with particularity so that the assured may know what case he or she has to meet. He or she is entitled to have the best particulars available in those circumstances, which the insurers will, by direct evidence or by inference, attempt to establish as constituting scuttling.

Delay: As a rule, the insurer is not liable for damage caused by delay, though the delay results from a peril insured against. But difficult cases arise with regard to freight, especially as regards time charterers. When the venture is frustrated by a peril insured against, and freight is thereby lost, the insurer is liable.

Thus, when a ship was delayed by the operation of perils of the seas, and the charterer justifiably refused to load, it was held to be a loss of freight by "perils of the seas."

Loss of time freight, resulting from detention for repair of general average damage, is not allowed in general average.

9.56   Partial and Total Losses

1. A loss may be either total or partial. Any loss other than a total loss, as hereinafter defined, is a partial loss.
2. A loss may be either an actual total loss or a constructive total loss.
3. Unless a different intention appears from the terms of the policy, an insurance against total loss includes a constructive, as well as an actual total, loss.
4. Where the assured brings an action for a total loss, and the evidence proves only a partial loss, he or she may, unless the policy otherwise provides, recover for a partial loss.
5. Where goods reach their destination in specie, but by reason of obligation of marks or otherwise they are incapable of identification, the loss, if any, is partial and not total.

Note

A loss must be either total or partial. A total loss of part is a partial loss. For example, if one hundred bags of seed are insured, and ten are destroyed by perils insured against, this is a partial loss.

9.57 Actual Total Loss

1. Where the subject matter insured is destroyed or so damaged as to cease to be a thing of the kind insured, or where the assured is irretrievably deprived thereof, there is an actual total loss.
2. In the case of an actual total loss, no notice of abandonment need be given.

Note

Where, by a peril insured against them, the goods of different owners are damaged and become so inextricably mixed as to be incapable of identification, the loss is partial, not total.

Goods ceased to exist *in specie* when they no longer fell under the commercial denomination under which they were insured.

9.58 Missing Ship

Where the ship concerned in the venture is missing, and after the lapse of a reasonable time, no news of it has been received, an actual total loss may be presumed.

Note

Reasonable time is a question of fact.

If the insurer pays for a missing ship as lost, and afterward it turns up, it belongs to the insurer.

When a ship is missing in wartime, the court must consider the probabilities, and determine as best it can whether the loss falls on the marine or the war risk underwriters.

9.59 Effect of Transshipment and So Forth

Where, by a peril insured against, the voyage is interrupted at an intermediate port or place under such circumstances, apart from any special stipulation in the contract of affreightment, to justify the master in landing and reshipping the goods or other movables, or in transshipping them and sending them on to their destination, the liability of the insurer continues, notwithstanding the landing or transshipment.

Note

The English rules as to transshipment are not very well settled. In the United States and under some foreign codes, it is the duty of the master to transship whenever it is reasonable to do so.

When goods have to be landed and transshipped, the consequent expenses, according to the circumstances, are recoverable as general average and sometimes as particular charges. But to avoid difficulties of proof, policies on goods now commonly include a clause in which underwriters agree to pay landing, warehousing, and forwarding charges.

9.60 Constructive Total Loss

1. Subject to any express provision in the policy, there is a constructive total loss where the subject matter insured is

reasonably abandoned on account of its actual total loss appearing to be unavoidable, or because it could not be preserved from actual total loss without an expenditure that would exceed its value when the expenditure had been incurred.

2. In particular, there is a constructive total loss:

    (I)   Where the assured is deprived of the possession of his or her ship or goods by a peril insured against, and (a) it is unlikely that he or she can recover the ship or goods, as the case may be; or (b) the cost of recovering the ship or goods would exceed their value when recovered, or

    (II) In the case of damage to a ship, where it is so damaged by a peril insured against that the cost of repairing the damage would exceed the value of the ship when repaired.

In estimating the cost of repairs, no deduction is to be made in respect to general average contribution to those repairs payable by other interest, but an account is to be taken of the expense of future salvage operations and of any future general average contributions to which the ship would be liable if repaired; or

    (III) In the case of damage to goods, where the cost of repairing the damage and forwarding the goods to their destination would exceed their value on arrival.

Note

It is commonly said that, for the purpose of determining whether the assured is entitled to treat a loss as a constructive total loss, regard must be given to the course that would be pursued by a prudent uninsured owner in the circumstances of the case. When the test of the act by the prudent uninsured owner is applicable, the question is not what the particular owner, if uninsured, would do, but what a person of average prudence ought to do in similar circumstances.

Constructive total loss lies midway between actual total loss on the one hand and partial loss on the other. It is in effect a hybrid loss, and its dual character has complicated the decisions. In some instances, notice of abandonment has been given as a matter of precaution, and a case is treated as one of constructive total loss when the facts would have justified its being treated as an actual total loss. In other instances, due notice of abandonment has not been given, and the case has to be treated as a partial loss, though the facts show a constructive total loss.

In the majority of cases, the distinction between actual total loss and constructive total loss corresponds with the distinction that has been drawn between physical impossibility and business impossibility. A merchant trades for profit, not for pleasure, and the law will not compel him or her to carry on business at a loss.

In practice, a clause in the policy usually states that "in ascertaining whether the vessel is a constructive total loss, the insured value shall be taken as the repaired value, and nothing in respect to the damaged or breakup value or wreck shall be taken into account."

Loss of voyage: There may be a loss of the goods by a loss of the voyage in which the goods are being transported, if it amounts to the destruction of the contemplated venture.

In the United States, unless the policy otherwise provides, there is a constructive total loss if the damage to a ship exceeds 50 percent of its repaired value.

The rules as to constructive total loss are specific to marine insurance and do not apply to nonmarine policies.

9.61 Effect of Constructive Total Loss

Where there is a constructive total loss, the assured may either treat the loss as a partial loss or abandon the subject matter insured to the insurer and treat the loss as if it were an actual total loss.

Note

A constructive total loss is when the damage is of such a character that the assured is entitled, if he or she thinks fit, to treat it as a total loss.

Abandonment: The act does not define "abandonment," and the term is used in different senses.

First, and strictly, in the case of a constructive total loss, it denotes the voluntary cession by the assured to the insurer of whatever remains of the subject matter insured, together with all proprietary rights and remedies in respect thereof. This is the meaning in which it is used in the act.

Secondly, but incorrectly, it is used as equivalent to notice or tender of abandonment, such as the act by which the assured signifies to the insurer his or her election to abandon what remains and to claim for a total loss.

Thirdly, it denotes the cession or transfer, which takes place, by operation of law, of whatever remains of the subject matter insured when the insurer pays for a total loss. In this sense, it is a corollary of the doctrine of subrogation, which is a necessary incident of every contract of indemnity.

9.62 Notice of Abandonment

1. Subject to the provisions of this section, where the assured elects to abandon the subject matter insured to the insurer,

he or she must give notice of abandonment. If he or she fails to do so, the loss can only be treated as a partial loss.

2. Notice of abandonment may be given in writing or by word of mouth or partly in writing and partly by word of mouth, and it may be given in any terms that indicate the intention of the assured to abandon his or her insured interest in the subject matter unconditionally to the insurer.

3. Notice of abandonment must be given with reasonable diligence after the receipt of reliable information of the loss, but where the information is of a doubtful character, the assured is entitled to a reasonable time to make inquiry.

4. Where notice of abandonment is properly given, the rights of the assured are not prejudiced by the fact that the insurer refuses to accept the abandonment.

5. The acceptance of an abandonment may be either expressly stated or implied by the insurer. The mere silence of the insurer after notice is not an acceptance.

6. Where notice of abandonment is accepted, the abandonment is irrevocable. The acceptance of the notice conclusively admits liability for the loss and the sufficiency of the notice.

7. Notice of abandonment is unnecessary where, at the time when the assured receives information of the loss, there would be no possibility of benefit to the insurer if notice were given to him or her.

8. Notice of abandonment may be waived by the insurer.

9. Where an insurer has reinsured his or her risk, no notice of abandonment need be given by him or her.

Note

Suppose notice of abandonment is given, and the insurer does not accept it. Can the assured withdraw the notice? An English judge answered this question by saying that "by a notice of abandonment, the assured merely makes an offer, which remains executor unless and until it is accepted. Until it is accepted, the assured has the right to look to intervening events that may restore in whole or in part his or her former situation, and he or she may limit this claim accordingly if it suits him or her better to claim for a partial loss.

It seems that, where due notice of abandonment has not been given, the right to give notice of abandonment may revive on a change of circumstance.

Notice of abandonment is not excused simply because the insurers, if notified, could have done nothing more than was done by the assured. If the goods are there to be dealt with, and there is something useful that can be done, notice must be given.

"Information of the loss" means information such that the assured is in a position to make up his or her mind that there is a constructive total loss.

Notice of abandonment can only be given by or on behalf of the owner of the subject matter insured. It cannot be given by a pledge of the policy, but it can be given by a joint owner who manages the vessel for the rest.

9.63   Effect of Abandonment

1. Where there is a valid abandonment, the insurer is entitled to take over the interest of the assured in whatever may remain of the subject matter insured, and all proprietary rights incidental thereto.
2. Upon the abandonment of a ship, the insurer thereof is entitled to any freight in course of being earned, and that

is earned by it subsequent to the casualty causing the loss, less the expenses of earning it incurred after the casualty; and where the ship is carrying the owner's goods, the insurer is entitled to a reasonable remuneration for the carriage of them subsequent to the casualty causing the loss.

Note

When the total loss of a thing insured is not actual but constructive (that is, where the thing insured is *in specie*, but the cost of preserving and repairing it would be more than its value when preserved or repaired), the assured must give a notice of abandonment. This in itself does not pass any property or rights in the thing insured to the underwriter. If the underwriter then pays the assured a total loss, it used to be thought that the payment passed the property and rights incidental to it to the underwriter, as benefit of salvage.

It has been suggested that, in case of abandonment, freight should be apportioned between the insurer on ship and the insurer on freight.

The provisions of this section may be modified by agreement. They are modified, for example, by clause 18 of the Institute Time Clauses—Hulls, which states: "In the event of total loss or constructive total loss, no claim to be made by the underwriters for freight, whether notice of abandonment has been given or not."

On abandonment, any action performed subsequent to the casualty causing the loss by the assured or his or her agents for the protection of the subject matter insured is at the risk of the insurer and for his or her benefit, provided such an act is done in good faith and reasonably.

Partial Loss (Including Salvage and General Average and Particular Charges)
9.64   Particular Average Loss

1. A particular average loss is a partial loss of the subject matter insured caused by a peril insured against and that is not a general average loss.
2. Expenses incurred by or on behalf of the assured for the safety or preservation of the subject matter insured, other than general average and salvage charges, are called "particular charges." Particular charges are not included in particular average.

Note

A general average differs from a particular average in its nature and incidence. General average is a partial loss, voluntarily incurred for the common safety, and made good proportionally by all parties concerned in the adventure. Particular average is a partial loss, fortuitously caused by a maritime peril, and that has to be borne by the party upon whom it falls.

Where there is a general average loss, the period of limitation under the Limitation Act of 1980 runs from the date of the loss, and not from the date when the average statement prepared by the average adjuster is published to the insurers.

9.65   Salvage Charges

1. Subject to any express provision in the policy, salvage charges incurred in preventing a loss by perils insured against may be recovered as a loss by those perils.
2. Salvage charges means the charges recoverable under maritime law by a salver independently of contract. They do not include the expenses of services in the nature of

salvage rendered by the assured or his or her agent, or any person employed for hire by them, for the purpose of averting a peril insured against. Such expenses, where properly incurred, may be covered as particular charges or as a general average loss, according to the circumstances under which they were incurred.

Note

Salvage charges are recoverable under the policy, and not under the "sue and labor" clause. They cannot be recovered in addition to the sum insured, but the total liability of the insurer is limited to the sum insured.

The expression "salvage" in maritime law is applied to the salver's services and salver's reward. It is used to denote the services of a salver who intervenes voluntarily and whose rights are given him or her by maritime law, and it is also used to denote the services of a salver who is employed by the ship and whose rights depend on contract. In insurance law, it is also used to denote the thing saved, as for instance, in the phrase "without benefit of salvage," or when a loss is referred to as a "salvage loss."

9.66   General Average Loss

1. A general average loss is a loss caused by or directly consequential on a general average act. It includes a general average expenditure as well as a general average sacrifice.
2. There is a general average act where any extraordinary sacrifice or expenditure is voluntarily and reasonably made or incurred in time of peril for the purpose of preserving the property implied in the common venture.
3. Where there is a general average loss, the party on whom it falls is entitled, subject to the conditions imposed by

maritime law, to a ratable contribution from the other parties interested, and such a contribution is called a general average contribution.

4. Subject to any express provision in the policy, where the assured has incurred a general average expenditure, he or she may recover from the insurer in respect to the proportion of the loss that falls upon him; and in the case of general average sacrifice, he or she may recover from the insurer in respect to the whole loss without having enforced his or her right of contribution from the other parties liable to contribute.

5. Subject to any express provision in the policy, where the assured has paid, or is liable to pay, a general average contribution in respect to the subject matter insured, he or she may recover therefore from the insurer.

6. In the absence of express stipulation, the insurer is not liable for any general average loss or contribution where the loss was not incurred for the purpose of avoiding, or in connection with the avoidance of, a peril insured against.

7. Where ship, freight, and cargo, or any two of those interests, are owned by the same assured, the liability of the insurer in respect to general average losses or contributions is to be determined as if those subjects were covered by the different persons.

Note

"General average" is defined as follows: "all losses that arise in consequence of extraordinary sacrifice made, or expenses incurred, for the preservation of the ship and cargo come within general average, and must be borne proportionally by all who are interested."

The obligation to contribute in general average exists between the parties to the adventure, whether they are insured or not. The circumstances of a party being insured can have no influence on the adjustment of general average. If a contributing party is insured, he or she can claim an indemnity against the underwriter in respect to the contribution that he or she has been compelled to pay in general average.

It is the duty of shipowner and the shipowner's agents to take such steps as may be reasonable to provide that all general average contributions (whether due to himself or others) are adjusted and collected, and he or she has a lien on the cargo until this is done.

Measure of Indemnity
9.67   Extent of Liability of Insurer for Loss

1. The sum that the assured can recover in respect to a loss on a policy by which he or she is insured, in the case of an unvalued policy, to the full extent of the insurable value, or, in a valued policy, to the full extent of the value fixed by the policy, is called the measure of indemnity.
2. Where there is a loss recoverable under the policy, the insurer, or each insurer, if there be more than one, is liable for such proportion of the measure of indemnity as the amount of his or her subscription bears to the value fixed by the policy, in the case of a valued policy, or to the insurable value in the case of an unvalued policy.

Note

Insurance is a contract of indemnity, but in marine insurance, the amount of the proceeds (assuming that the subject matter is insured) is fully covered by insurance. Suppose a ship valued at US$100,000 is insured for only US$10,000. The shipowner is said to be his or her "own insurer" for $90,000, and any loss that occurs must be adjusted on this basis.

THE MARINE INSURANCE HANDBOOK

9.68   Total Loss

Subject to the provisions of this act and to any express provision in the policy, where there is a total loss of the subject matter insured:

1. if the policy be a valued policy, the measure of indemnity is the sum fixed by the policy, or
2. if the policy be an unvalued policy, the measure of indemnity is the insurable value of the subject matter insured.

Note

Valued and unvalued policies were discussed in sections 27 and 28, and "insurable value" was discussed in section 16.

9.69   Partial Loss of a Ship

Where a ship is damaged but is not totally lost, the measure of indemnity, subject to any express provision in the policy, is as follows:

1. Where the ship has been repaired, the assured is entitled to the reasonable cost of the repairs, less the customary deductions, but not exceeding the sum insured in respect to any one casualty.
2. Where the ship has been only partially repaired, the assured is entitled to the reasonable cost of such repairs, computed as above, and also to be indemnified for the reasonable depreciation, if any, arising from the unrepaired damage, provided that the aggregate amount shall not exceed the cost of repairing the whole damage, computed as above.
3. Where the ship has not been repaired and has not been sold in its damaged state during the risk, the assured is entitled to be indemnified for the reasonable

163

depreciation arising from the unrepaired damage, but not exceeding the reasonable cost of repairing such damage computed as above.

Note

It was decided in an English court in a case where the ship is not repaired but sold in its damaged state during the risk that the assured was entitled to the reasonable cost of repairing such damage, not exceeding the actual depreciation in the value of the ship as ascertained by the sale.

What was to be taken as the basis of depreciation if a ship were sold in its damaged state? The sale price is one factor, so is the value of the ship at the commencement of risk and/or at time of casualty.

In the case of a time policy at which the measure of indemnity falls, the time when the policy expires is to be determined. It is only when the risk is ended that it can be predicted for certain that neither repair nor sale will take place during the risk.

Where a ship is not repaired or sold during the risk, the measure of indemnity is the depreciation (not exceeding the reasonable cost of repairs) arising from the unrepaired damage. But where the damaged value of a vessel is virtually zero, the indemnity is limited to the reasonable cost of the repairs.

Section 69(3) requires the measure of indemnity to be quantified on the basis of what it would have cost to repair a vessel if the repairs had been carried out. Thus, if it would have been necessary for it to be towed to a port for repairs, the cost of towing, although not incurred, is recoverable as part of the partial-loss claim.

9.70 Partial Loss of Freight

Subject to any express provision in the policy, where there is a partial loss of freight, the measure of indemnity is such a proportion of the sum fixed by the policy in the case of valued policy, or of the insurable value in the case of an unvalued policy, as the proportion of freight lost by the assured bears to the whole freight at the risk of the assured under the policy.

Note

The insurable value in the case of freight is the gross freight. The rule for adjusting a partial loss on freight is that, where the sum insured is less than the value of the interest at risk, the underwriter pays the same proportional part of the loss that the sum insured is of the insurable value of the fright; if the sum insured equals the insurable value of the interest, then he or she pays the whole of the loss.

9.71 Partial Loss of Goods and Merchandise

Where there is a partial loss of goods, merchandise, or other movables, the measure of indemnity, subject to any express provision in the policy, is as follows:

1. Where part of the goods, merchandise, or other movables insured by a valued policy is totally lost, the measure of indemnity is such a proportion of the sum fixed by the policy as the insurable value of the part lost bears to the insurable value of the whole, ascertained as in the case of an unvalued policy.
2. Where part of the goods, merchandise, or other movables insured by an unvalued policy is totally lost, the measure of indemnity is the insurable value of the part lost, ascertained as in the case of total loss.

3. Where the whole of any part of the goods or merchandise insured has been delivered damaged at its destination, the measure of indemnity is such proportion of the sum fixed by the policy, in the case of a valued policy, or of the insurable value in the case of an unvalued policy, as the difference between the gross sound and damaged values at the place of arrival bears to the gross sound value.

4. The term "gross value" denotes the wholesale price, or, if there be no such price, the estimated value with, in either case, freight, landing charges, and duty paid beforehand, provided that in the case of goods or merchandise customarily sold in bond, the bonded price is deemed to be the gross value. "Gross proceeds" refers to the actual price obtained at a sale where all charges at the sale are paid by the sellers.

Note

The insurers insure against actual damage to the goods but not against prejudice or suspicion of damage. However great the suspicion of damage and however strong the moral belief and conviction of the assured, unless damage is proved on the balance of probabilities on the basis of legal evidence and material on record, there cannot be proof of damage.

9.72 Apportionment of Valuation

1. Where different species of property are insured under a single valuation, the valuation must be apportioned over the different species in proportion to their respective insurable values, as in the case of an unvalued policy. The insured value of any part of a species is such proportion of the total insured value of the

same as the insurable value of the part bears to the insurable value of the whole ascertained in both cases as provided by this act.

2. Where a valuation has to be apportioned, and particulars of the prime cost of each separate species, quality, or description of goods cannot be ascertained, the division of the valuation may be made over the net arrived values of the different species, qualities, or description of goods.

Note

"Insurable value" was discussed in section 16(3), and the mode of ascertaining the value referred to in subsection (1) was discussed in section 71, as read with section 16.

9.73 General Average Contribution and Salvage Charges

1. Subject to any express provision in the policy, where the assured has paid or is liable for any general average contribution, the measure of indemnity is the full amount of such contribution if the subject matter liable to contribution is insured for its full contributory value; but if such subject matter be not insured for its full contributory value, or if only part of it be insured, the indemnity payable by the insurer must be reduced in proportion to the under insurance, and where there has been a particular-average loss that constitutes a deduction from the contributory value and for which the insurer is liable, that amount must be deducted from the insured value in order to ascertain what the insurer is liable to contribute.

2. Where the insurer is liable for salvage charges, the extent of his or her liability must be determined on the like principle.

Note

Suppose goods are insured for US$1,500 by a valued policy. General average is incurred, of which eighty dollars is found to be the proportion payable by the owner of the goods, their contributory value being taken at $1,600. The insurer is liable for fifteen-sixteenths of eighty dollars, i.e., seventy-five dollars. But if the contributory value of the goods is taken at $1,500, the insurer is liable for the whole eighty dollars.

9.74 Liabilities to Third Parties

Where the assured has effected an insurance in express terms against any liability to a third party, the measure of indemnity, subject to any express provision in the policy, is the amount paid or payable by him or her to such third party in respect to such liability.

Note

An insurance against liability to a third person is a distinct engagement added to the ordinary policy.

In a case where it was held that the "sue and labor" clause in the policy could not be read in connection with the "running down" clause so as to supplement it, the court, speaking of the latter, said, "It is in each case a special contract very different from the contract of insurance in its ordinary form; and the liability under it does not depend upon the ordinary perils covered by the policy, but upon the special matters mentioned in the clause itself."

The insurer is liable under the ordinary form of policy for damage caused by collision to the assured's ship, whether it is at fault or not. The construction of a "collision" or "running down" clause depends entirely on the language used by the parties in the particular clause in question.

9.75 General Provisions as to Measure of Indemnity

1. Where there has been a loss in respect to any subject matter not expressly provided for in the foregoing provisions of this act, the measure of indemnity shall be ascertained, as nearly as may be, in accordance with those provisions, insofar as applicable to the particular case.
2. Nothing in the provisions of this act relating to the measure of indemnity shall affect the rules relating to double insurance, or prohibit the insurer from disproving interest wholly or in part, or from showing that at the time of the loss, the whole or any part of the subject matter insured was not at risk under the policy.

Note

If the provisions of subsection (1) do not meet the case, recourse may be had under common law.

9.76 Particular Average Warranties

1. Where the subject matter insured is warranted free from particular average, the assured cannot recover for a loss of part, other than a loss incurred by a general average sacrifice, unless the contract contained in the policy be apportionable, but if the contract be apportionable, the assured may recover for a total loss of any apportionable part.

2. Where the subject matter insured is warranted free from particular average, either wholly or under a certain percentage, the insurer is nevertheless liable for salvage charges and for particular charges and other expenses properly incurred pursuant to the provisions of the suing and laboring clause in order to avert a loss insured against.
3. Unless the policy otherwise provides, where the subject matter insured is warranted free from particular average under a specified percentage, a general average loss cannot be added to a particular average loss to make up the specified percentage.
4. For the purpose of ascertaining whether the specified percentage has been reached, regard shall be had only to the actual loss suffered by the subject matter insured. Particular charges and the expenses of and incidental to ascertaining and proving the loss must be excluded.

Note

A policy, or rather, the contract contained in it, is apportionable where the policy itself provides for apportionment, or where, by usage, it is treated as apportionable.

The particular average warranty is sometimes spoken of as a franchise. Thus, if a ship, warranted free from average under 3 percent, is damaged to the extent of 5 percent, the assured is entitled to recover the whole 5 percent.

In the case of a voyage policy, successive losses may be added to make up the specified percentage.

In the case of a time policy, successive losses on the same voyage may be added together, but losses occurring on different voyages cannot be added together to make up the specified percentage.

THE MARINE INSURANCE HANDBOOK

9.77   Successive Losses

1. Unless the policy otherwise provides, and subject to the provisions of this act, the insurer is liable for successive losses, even though the total amount of such losses may exceed the sum insured.
2. Where, under the same policy, a partial loss that has not been repaired or otherwise made good is followed by a total loss, the assured can only recover in respect to the total loss, provided that nothing in this section shall affect the liability of the insurer under the suing and laboring clause.

Note

It is clear that whenever the underwriter adjusts a partial loss, he or she still remains liable under the policy and may go on paying partial losses exceeding in the whole cent percent and may ultimately have to pay a total loss of cent percent.

9.78   Suing and Laboring Clause

1. Where the policy contains a suing and laboring clause, the engagement thereby entered into is deemed to be supplementary to the contract of insurance, and the assured may recover from the insurer any expenses properly incurred pursuant to the clause, notwithstanding that the insurer may have paid for a total loss, or that the subject matter may have been warranted free from particular average, either wholly or under certain percentage.
2. General average losses and contributions and salvage charges, as defined by this act, are not recoverable under the suing and laboring clause.

3. Expenses incurred for the purpose of averting or diminishing any loss not covered by the policy are not recoverable under the suing and laboring clause.
4. It is the duty of the assured and his or her agents, in all cases, to take measures as may be reasonable for the purpose of averting or minimizing a loss.

Note

The assured and his or her agents are bound by law to use all reasonable efforts to avert or minimize a loss. The "sue and labor" clause enables the assured to recover the expenditure involved in these efforts from the insurer.

The sue and labor clause is usually supplemented by the "waiver clause," which provides that no acts of the insurer in recovering, saving, or preserving the property insured shall be considered as a waiver or acceptance of abandonment.

Although the sue and labor clause is a distinct engagement added to the policy, expenses incurred under it are apportioned according to the normal rule of marine insurance.

Where there is no sue and labor clause in the policy, particular charges incurred by the assured in preserving the subject matter insured may be recoverable.

Right of Insurer on Payment
9.79   Right of Subrogation

1. Where the insurer pays for a total loss, either of the whole, or in the case of goods of any apportionable part, of the subject matter insured, he or she thereupon becomes entitled to take over the interest of the assured in whatever may remain of the subject matter

so paid for, and he or she is thereby subrogated to all the rights and remedies of the assured in respect to that subject matter as from the time of the casualty causing the loss.

2. Subject to the foregoing provisions, where the insurer pays for a partial loss, he or she acquires no title to the subject matter insured, or such part of it as may remain, but is thereupon subrogated to all rights and remedies of the assured in and in respect to the subject matter insured as from the time of the casualty causing the loss, insofar as the assured has been indemnified, according to this act, by such payment for the loss.

Note

The right of subrogation is a necessary incident of a contract of indemnity, and it operates on every right and remedy "by which the loss insured against can be or has been diminished." If the assured is indemnified, it was formerly suggested that the insurer might recover from a third party more than he or she had paid. But it has now been definitely decided that this is not so, and that the insurer cannot recover under the doctrine of subrogation more than he or she has paid.

The question has been raised whether an insurer, merely by paying for a total loss, becomes the "owner" of the thing insured. It will be noted that section 79(1) provides that the insurer becomes "entitled to take over" the interest of the assured.

The right of subrogation may be waived by agreement between the assured and the insurer. Further, the policy may contain an implied term that the insurer will not exercise the right of subrogation.

9.80   Right of Contribution

1. Where the assured is overinsured by double insurance, each insurer is bound as between himself or herself and the other insurers, to contribute ratably to the loss in proportion to the amount for which he or she is liable under the contract.
2. If any insurer pays more than his or her proportion of the loss, he or she is entitled to maintain an action for contribution against the other insurers and is entitled to the like remedies as a surety who has paid more than his or her proportion of debt.

Note

Coinsurers are not cosureties, but in many respects, they have similar relations *inter se*. When two or more policies are effected on the same subject matter and interest, "the policies are one insurance as between all the underwriters, but not one insurance for all purposes."

9.81   Effect of Underinsurance

Where the assured is insured for an amount less than the insurable value, or, in the case of a valued policy, for an amount less than the policy valuation, the assured is deemed to be his or her own insurer in respect to the uninsured balance.

Note

The measure of indemnity rests on the hypothesis that the subject matter insured is to be regarded as fully insured.

Suppose a ship valued at US$3,000 is insured with "A" for $1,000 and with "B" for $1,000. If it is damaged by perils of the seas to the extent of $300, "A" is liable for $100, and B is liable for $100. That being so, it is obviously immaterial to "A" and "B" whether the remaining $1,000 is uninsured or whether it is insured with "C."

Return of Premium
9.82   Enforcement of Return

Where the premium or a proportionate part thereof is, by this act, declared to be returnable:

a) if already paid, it may be recovered by the assured from the insurer, and
b) if unpaid, it may be retained by the assured or his or her agent.

Note

The broker is directly responsible to the insurer for the payment of the premium, but when returnable, it is repayable to the assured.

9.83   Return by Agreement

Where the policy contains a stipulation for the return of premium, or a proportionate part thereof, on the happening of a certain event, and that event happens, the premium, or as the case may be, the proportionate part thereof, is thereupon returnable to the assured.

Note

Clause 21 of the Institute Time Clauses—Hulls states the rate for return of premium in cases of cancelation or laid up or for repair or at port.

Similarly, cargo policies may contain return of premium in case of "no claim."

9.84 Return for Failure of Consideration

1. Where the consideration for the payment of the premium totally fails, and there has been no fraud or illegality on the part of the assured or his or her agents, the premium is thereupon returnable to the assured.
2. Where the consideration for the payment of the premium is apportionable and there is a total failure of any apportionable part of the consideration, a proportionate part of the premium is, under the like conditions, thereupon returnable to the assured.
3. In particular:
   a. Where the policy is void or is voided by the insurer as from the commencement of the risk, the premium is returnable, provided that there has been no fraud or illegality on the part of the assured; but if the risk is not apportionable and has once attached, the premium is not returnable.
   b. Where the subject matter insured, or part thereof, has never been imperiled, the premium, or as the case may be, a proportionate part thereof, is returnable.

Provided that where the subject matter has been insured "lost or not lost," and has arrived in safety at the time when the contract is concluded, the premium is not returnable unless at such time the insurer knew of the safe arrival.

   a) Where the assured has no insurable interest throughout the currency of the risk, the premium is returnable, provided that this rule does not apply to a policy effected by way of gaming or wagering.
   b) Where the assured has a defeasible interest that is terminated during the currency of the risk, the premium is not returnable.

c) Where the assured has overinsured under an unvalued policy, a proportionate part of the premium is returnable.

d) Subject to the foregoing provisions, where the assured has overinsured by double insurance, a proportionate part of the several premiums is returnable.

Provided that, if the policies are effected at different times, and any earlier policy has at any time borne the entire risk, or if a claim has been paid on the policy in respect to the full sum insured thereby, no premium is returnable in respect to that policy, and when the double insurance is effected knowingly by the assured, no premium is returnable.

Note

The return of premium rests on the doctrine of failure of consideration.

The general rule of law is that, where a contract has been in part performed, no part of the money paid under such contract can be recovered back. There may be some cases of partial performance that form exceptions to this rule, as, for instance, if there were a contract to deliver ten sacks of wheat only and six were delivered, the price of the remaining four might be recovered back. But there, the consideration is clearly severable.

The case of double insurance gives rise to complications. The assured has the right to elect under which policy or set of policies he or she will claim for a loss and under which policy or set of policies he or she will claim for a return of premium, but the underwriters, having settled with the assured, must proceed to readjust the entire claim among themselves, so that each underwriter shall ultimately bear his or her proportionate part both of the loss and the return premium.

Mutual Insurance
9.85   Modification of Act in Case of Mutual Insurance

1. Where two or more persons mutually agree to insure each other against marine losses, there is said to be a mutual insurance.
2. The provisions of this act relating to the premium do not apply to mutual insurance, but a guarantee or such other arrangement as may be agreed upon may be substituted for the premium.
3. The provisions of this act insofar as they may be modified by the agreement of the parties may in the case of mutual insurance be modified by the terms of the policies issued by the association or by the rules and regulations of the association.
4. Subject to the exceptions mentioned in this section, the provisions of this act apply to a mutual insurance.

Note

Mutual insurance is a system by which everyone insured is at once both underwriter and assured. This very simple principle was acted upon successfully for many years until technical difficulties began to be interposed. The first technical difficulty was this: all mutual insurance associations were ordered by statute to be incorporated as joint stock companies. The second technical difficulty was that, under statutes framed for different purposes, which were positive in their terms, every contract of insurance had to be recorded in a written document; there must be a policy of insurance. These two conditions have to be complied with, and the mutual insurance associations set themselves to work by various forms of rules to endeavor to reconcile the rules of the law with the conduct of their business, and different regulations have been adopted to meet the decisions on the subject.

The policies issued by mutual insurance associations to members omit the ordinary provisions regarding premiums. The omission is provided for by rules of the association, which regulates members' contributions to losses.

Supplemental
9.86   Ratification by Assured

Where a contract of marine insurance is in good faith effected by one person on behalf of another, the person on whose behalf it is effected may ratify the contract even after he or she is aware of a loss.

Note

This is an old rule of marine law. This is a legitimate exception from the general rule, because the case is not within the principle of that rule. Where an agent effects an insurance subject to ratification, the loss is very likely to happen before ratification, and it must be taken that the insurance so effected involves that possibility as the basis of the contract.

The insurance can only be ratified by the person on whose behalf it is effected.

9.87   Implied Obligation Varied by Agreement or Usage

1. Where any right, duty, or liability would arise under a contract of marine insurance by implication of law, it may be negative or varied by express agreement or by usage if the usage be such as to bind both parties to the contract.
2. The provisions of this section extend to any right, duty, or liability declared by this act, which may be lawfully modified by agreement.

Note

Marine insurance is a consensual contract, and in the absence of a positive legal prohibition, the parties may make any stipulation they please.

The main object of the act is to declare the law: to indicate to the parties the legal position if they do not make any express bargain, leaving them free to make any bargain they like to suit their own needs.

9.88 Reasonable Time: A Question of Fact

Whereby this act any reference is made to reasonable time, reasonable premium, or reasonable diligence, the question of what is reasonable is a question of fact.

Note

What is "reasonable" is what a person or group of persons would decide in certain circumstances.

9.89 Slip as Evidence

Where there is a duly stamped policy, reference may be made, as heretofore, to the slip or covering note in any legal proceeding.

Note

The slip is clearly a contract of marine insurance and is equally clearly not a policy; it may be given in evidence wherever it is, though not valid material.

THE MARINE INSURANCE HANDBOOK

The "slip" cannot be used to contradict the terms of the policy unless there is a clear case of common mistake. It may then be used for the purpose of rectifying the policy.

9.90 Interpretation of Terms

In this act, unless the contract or subject matter otherwise requires:

"Action" includes counterclaim and setoff;

"Freight" includes the profit derivable by a shipowner from the employment of his or her ship to carry the shipowner's own goods or movables, as well as freight payable by a third party, but it does not include passage money;

"Movables" includes any movable tangible property, other than the ship, and includes money, valuable securities, and other documents; and

"Policy" denotes a marine policy.

Note

"Action": This definition is merely inclusive.

"Freight": In shipping law, the term "freight" is sometimes used to denote the goods or cargo onboard a ship. More usually, it is used to denote the sum payable to a shipowner by a third person for the use of a ship as a vehicle for merchandise.

"Movables": In commercial law generally, the term "goods" includes all movable tangible property, but in marine

181

insurance law, the term has a restricted meaning, which requires this definition.

"Policy": Sections 1, 2, and 22 refer to a "marine policy."

9.91   Savings

1. Nothing in this act, or in any repeal effected thereby, shall affect the following:
    a) The provisions of the Stamp Act of 1891 or any enactment for the time being in force relating to the revenue
    b) The provisions of the Companies Act of 1862 or any enactment amending or substituted for the same
    c) The provisions of any statute not expressly repealed by this act
2. The provisions of the common law, including the law merchant (save insofar as they are inconsistent with the express provisions of this act) shall continue to apply to contracts of marine insurance.

Note

In England, as in the United States, the marine and commercial cases are dealt with by the ordinary courts of justice. The Law Merchant is part of the Common Law, and its special rules are enforced as part of the ordinary law of the land. Marine insurance is a contract, and insofar as the contract has not special incidents peculiar to itself, it is dealt with on the same footing as other contracts.

9.92 And 93: These Sections Were Replaced by the Statute Law Revision Act of 1927

9.94 Short Title

This act may be cited as the Marine Insurance Act of 1906.

Note

The act is concluded by the above section and must be read subject to the provisions of the Interpretation Act of 1978.

Where an act is divided into parts or headings, regard should be given to these divisions in construing the act.

CHAPTER 10

INTERNATIONAL CONVENTIONS

The United Nations organizations worked for the issue of unified rules to govern the obligations, liabilities, and duties of parties to contract of carriage by sea, air, road, or rail. The main purpose of these rules is to minimize possible disputes between the contracting parties who are located in different countries and are subject to different jurisdictions. These rules were issued and, if signed by a specific number of countries called signatories, shall be adopted in the legal system of these countries in which carriage commences or terminates in one of them.

The latest of these conventions are as follows:

10.1 The Rotterdam Conventions of 2008

The United Nations Convention for the international carriage of goods wholly or partly by sea establishes a uniform and modern legal regime governing the rights and obligations of shippers, carriers, and consignees under a contract for door-to-door carriage that includes an international sea leg.

The rules provide a modern alternative to earlier conventions relating to the international carriage of goods by sea, the following in particular:

1. Hague Rules of 1924
2. Hague-Visby Rules
3. Hamburg Rules of 1978

Some countries are still applying an older form depending on their status as exporter or importer of goods. The Rotterdam Conventions had raised the limit of liability of the carrier which is not accepted by some world shipping industries.

10.1.1 Transport Document
The bill of lading is the internationally accepted document issued under a contract of carriage by the carrier that:

1. evidences the carrier's or a performing party's receipt of goods under a contract of carriage, and
2. evidences or contains a contract of carriage.
3. issued to a named consignee or to the order if the bill is negotiable

10.1.2 Negotiable Transport Document
A transport document indicates by wording such as "to order" or "negotiable" or other appropriate wording recognized as having the same effect by the law applicable to the document that the goods have been consigned to the order of the shipper, to the order of the consignee, or to the bearer and is not explicitly stated as being "nonnegotiable or "not-negotiable."

10.1.3 Nonnegotiable Transport Document
This is a transport document that is not a negotiable document.

10.1.4 Carriage and Delivery of the Goods:
The carrier shall, subject to this convention and in accordance with the terms of contract of carriage, carry the goods to the

place of destination and deliver them to the consignee with due diligence to ensure safety of the goods during carriage.

10.1.5 Period of Responsibility of the Carrier

The period of responsibility of the carrier for the goods under this convention begins when the carrier or a performing party receives the goods for carriage and ends when the goods are relieved.

a. If the law or regulations of the *place of receipt* require the goods to be handed over to an authority or other third party from which the carrier may collect them, the period of responsibility of the carrier begins when the carrier collects the goods from the authority or other third party.

b. If the law or regulations of the *place of delivery* require the carrier to hand over the goods to an authority or other third party from which the consignee may collect them, the period of responsibility of the carrier ends when the carrier hands the goods to the authority or other third party.

10.1.6 Specific Obligations Applicable to the Voyage by Sea

Under the applicable rules,the carrier is bound before and during the voyage by sea to execute due diligence to:

a) make and keep the ship seaworthy;

b) properly crew, equip, and supply the ship and keep the ship so crewed, equipped, and supplied throughout the voyage; and

c) make and keep the holds and all other parts of the ship in which the goods are carried, and any containers supplied by the carrier, fit and safe for reception, carriage, and preservation.

10.1.7 Liability of the Carrier
Loss or Damage

1. The carrier is liable for loss of or damage to the goods as well as for delay in delivery if the claimant proves that the loss, damage, or delay or the event or circumstances that caused or contributed to it took place during the period of the carrier's responsibility.
2. The carrier is relieved of all or part of its liability pursuant to paragraph 1 if it proves that the cause or one of the causes of the loss, damage, or delay is not attributable to its fault.
3. The carrier is relieved of all or part of its liability pursuant to paragraph 1 if,   it proves that one or more of the following events or circumstances caused or contributed to the loss, damage, or delay:
   a. Acts of God
   b. Perils, dangers, and accidents of the sea or other navigable waters
   c. War, hostilities, armed conflict, piracy, terrorism, riots, and civil commotions
   d. Quarantine restrictions
   e. Strikes, lockouts, stoppage, or restraint of labor
   f. Fire on ship unless proved to be due to fault or negligence of carrier or their employees
   g. Latent defects not discoverable by due diligence.
   h. Acts or omission of the shipper
   i. Loading, handling, stowing, or unloading of the goods, unless the carrier or a performing party performs such activity on behalf of the shipper, the documentary shipper, or the consignee
   j. Wastage in bulk or weight or any other loss or damage arising from inherent defect, quality, or vice of the goods
   k. Insufficiency or defective condition of packing or marking not performed by or on behalf of the carrier

Delay

Delay in delivery occurs when the goods are not delivered at the place and destination provided for in the contract of carriage within the time agreed.Carriers' liability is limited in case of proof that delay was casued due to their fault or negligence.

10.1.8   Calculation of Compensation

1. The compensation payable by the carrier for loss of or damage to the goods is calculated by reference to the value of such goods at the place and time of delivery.
2. The value of goods is fixed according to the commodity exchange price or, if there is no such price, according to their market price or, if there is no commodity exchange price or market price, by reference to the normal value of goods of the same kind and quality at the place of delivery.

10.1.9   Notice of Loss

Cargo owner or receiver give a notice of loss or damage to the goods to be delivered to the carrier or their agent at time of delivery, or, if loss or damage is not apparent, within seven working days at the place of delivery after the delivery of the goods.

Notice is waived if the goods were subject to a joint survey at time of delivery.

10.1.10   Contract Particulars

Contract of carriage (Bill of Ladinbg) or similar document should include:

THE MARINE INSURANCE HANDBOOK

a) Description of goods
b) Marks and numbers
c) Weight
d) Apparent order and condition of goods
e) Name and address of carrier
f) Date on which the carrier or performing party received the goods, when goods are loaded onboard the ship, or when the transport document was issued
g) Name and address of the consignee
h) Name of ship
i) Place of receipt and place of delivery
j) Port of loading and port of discharge

10.1.11 Limit of Liability

Carrier's liability per package or unit is 875 units of account or three units of account per kilogram of the gross weight of the goods, whichever amount is higher, except when value is declared by the shipper and included in the contract particulars.

Unit of account is denoted by the Special Drawing Rights as determined by the International Monetary Fund.

In case of delay, the carrier's liability is limited to an amount equivalent to two and one-half times the freight payable on the goods delayed.

10.1.12 Time for Suit

No judicial or arbitral proceedings in respect to claims or disputes arising from a breach of an obligation under this convention may be instituted after the expiry of a period of two years.

The period referred to in the above paragraph commences on the day on which the carrier has delivered the goods or on which no goods have been delivered.

10.2 Conventions for the Unification of Certain Rules Relating to International Carriage by Air

10.2.1 Warsaw Convention of 1924

This convention was adopted in 1924 and followed by a number of subsequent amendments, led to an increasingly complex international legal framework with different international legal instruments coexisting with one another.

The major provision of the Warsaw Convention concerns the monetary cap limiting air carriers liability. This was fixed by reference to the gold franc being

1. 125,000 gold francs (about $5,000) at the rate of exchange prevailing in 1929 for passenger injury or death,
2. 250 gold francs (about $10) per kilogram for loss or damage to cargo or registered luggage, and
3. 5,000 gold francs per passenger for unregistered luggage.

10.2.2 Hague Protocol of 1955

In 1955, a protocol was adopted in The Hague to amend the Warsaw Convention. The Hague Protocol doubled the monetary cap on the carrier's liability in respect to passenger injury or death from 125,000 to 250,000 gold francs. There was no other change for cargo or registered luggage.

10.2.3 Guadalajara Convention of 1961

This was supplementary to the Warsaw Convention.

10.2.4 Guatemala City Protocol of 1971

This protocol did not enter into force.

10.2.5 Montreal Conventions of 1999

The Montreal Convention represents the most modern international convention in the field. It consolidates the various earlier legal instruments into a single text and provides the basis for genuine uniformity of laws governing transportation by air.

Air transport is increasingly gaining in importance, both in terms of its contribution to global trade and in terms of its development dimension. Although in terms of weight, air carriage accounts for around 2 percent of all cargo moved at the global level, in terms of value, it is estimated to be on the proportion of air transport ranging from 33 percent to 40 percent of the world trade in merchandise.

10.2.6 Carrier's Liability

Carrier's liability, according to the Montreal Convention, is amended as follows:

a) 100,000 SDR for injury or death of passengers
b) 4,150 SDR for delay to passengers
c) Loss or delay to baggage is limited to 1,000 SDR for each passenger
d) SDR 17 per kg. for loss or damage to cargo

10.2.7 Airway Bill(AWB)

This is the most essential document issued in respect to the international carriage of cargo. The airway bill evidences the contract or agreement of international carriage between the parties and plays a central role in the liability regime. The airway bill should contain particulars of goods, weight, place of receipt and place of delivery, name of carrier and name and address of consignee or receiver. Other information are as per the data entered in the bill of lading.

10.2.8 Notice of Claim

In the case of damage, the person entitled to delivery must complain to the carrier after the discovery of the damage and at the latest within seven days from the date of receipt in the case of checked luggage and fourteen days from the date of receipt in the case of cargo. In case of delay, the complaint must be made at the latest within twenty-one days from the date on which the luggage or cargo has been placed at his or her disposal.

10.2.9 Limitation of Action

The right to damage shall be extinguished if an action is not brought within a period of two years reckoned from the date of arrival at the destination or from the date on which the aircraft ought to have arrived or from the date on which the carriage stopped.

10.3 International Carriage of Goods By Road: Cmr
10.3.1 The Origin of the CMR

In order to standardize the conditions governing the contract for the international carriage of goods by road, particularly with respect to the documents used for such carriage and to the carrier's liability, eight European states (Austria, France, Luxemburg, Poland, Sweden, Switzerland, West Germany, and Yugoslavia) signed the Convention on the Contract for the International Carriage of Goods by Road in May of 1956.

The convention is generally known for its French title, CMR (*Convention Relative au Contract de Transport International de Marchandises par Route*).

10.3.2 The Scope of the CMR

The CMR is limited to contracts to carry goods. Goods are not defined in the CMR. However, goods may narrowly be described to be "goods in the nature of merchandise."

10.3.3 Multimodal Transport

1. The CMR applies to only the road stage if there is carriage by road between two states followed by a sea stage without a land vehicle.
2. There is carriage by road entirely within state A, followed by transshipment and carriage by sea from state A to a port in state B (whether or not followed by road or rail carriage to final destination within state B). The CMR does not apply to any stage of the transport.
3. There is a movement of goods as the two above possibilities, except that the goods are carried by sea without being "unloaded from the vehicle" on which they underwent the first road stage. The CMR applies to the entire journey.

10.3.4 The Consignment Note

The CMR requires the issue of a consignment note, but the absence of a consignment note does not deprive the contract or the CMR of all effects.

10.3.5 Contents of the Consignment Note

The consignment note shall contain the following particulars:

a) Date of the consignment note and the place at which it is made out
b) Name and address of the sender
c) Name and address of the carrier
d) Place and date of taking over of the goods and the place designated for delivery
e) Name and address of the consignee
f) Description in common use of the nature of the goods and the method of packing, and in the case of dangerous goods, a generally recognized description
g) Number of packages and their special marks and numbers
h) Gross weight of the goods or their quantity otherwise expressed
i) Charges relating to the carriage
j) Requisite instructions for customs and other formalities
k) A statement that the carriage is subject to the provision of this convention

10.3.6   Liability of the Carrier

The carrier shall be liable for the total or partial loss of the goods and for damage thereto occurring between the time when he or she takes over the goods and the time of delivery, as well as for any delay in delivery.

Delay in delivery occurs when the goods have not been delivered within thirty days following the expiry of the agreed time limit, or if there is no agreed time limit, within sixty days from the time when the carrier took over the goods.

10.3.7   The Period of Limitation

The period of limitation for an action arising out of carriage under this convention shall be one year. Nevertheless, in the case of willful misconduct, the period of limitation shall be three years.

THE MARINE INSURANCE HANDBOOK

10.3.8 Limit of Carrier's Liability

The convention was amended to replace the unit of account from the gold franc to SDR in accordance with the Carriage of Air and Road Act of 1979.

The amended article read: "Compensation shall not exceed 8.33 units of account per kilogram of gross weight short. Compensation for delay shall not exceed the carriage charges."

The unit of account mentioned in this convention is the Special Drawing Rights (SDR) as defined by the International Monetary Fund.

Summary

Carrier's liability for loss or damage to goods

Rotterdam Convention (By Sea)	Montreal Convention (By Air)	CMR (By Road)
SDR 875 per pkg SDR 3 per kg	SDR 17 per kg	SDR 8.33 per kg

195

CHAPTER 11

PROTECTION AND INDEMNITY ASSOCIATIONS (P&I CLUBS)

P&I clubs are mutual associations established by shipowners and/or charterers to protect them from possible third-party liabilities claims for loss, damage or injury that they may be held liable and would jeopardize their financial standings without such protection.

These associations are commonly known as P&I clubs or P&I insurance to provide coverage for a list of risks that traditional insurers are reluctant to insure or may not be within the scope of their limits . The coverage includes third-party risks for damage caused to cargo during carriage, war risks, and risks of environmental damage, such as oil spills and pollution.

A P&I club is an oldest form of mutual insurance that provides risk pooling, information, and representation for its members who are also the founders. Historically, P&I club members were shipowners, ship operators, or demise charterers, but more recently, freight forwarders and warehouse operators have been able to join.

Premium"Call"

P&I club members pay a "call" instead of a premium that is paid by the assured to the insurance company. A call

THE MARINE INSURANCE HANDBOOK

(advance call) is a sum of money that is put into the club's pool. If, at the end of the year, there are still funds in the pool, each member will pay a reduced call the following year, but if the club has made major payouts, club members will immediately have to pay a further call (supplementary call) to replenish the pools. P&I clubs are non-profit association working for the shipowners, thereby eliminating the underwriter's loading for profit or and making P&I insurance less costly to meet the claim cost as well as administration expenses.

The first mutual association was The Shipowners' Mutual Protection Society, was formed in 1855 as a consequence of a court decision in 1836, which ruled that third party liabiulity is not within the scope of coverage of the ship insurance. The coverage of the mutual protection society is intended to compensate for loss of life, injuries, and collisions that were excluded from marine insurance policies. Similar associations were later formed within the United Kingdom, Scandinavia, Japan, and the United States.

In 1874, the risk of carrier liability for cargo carried by the insured ship was added to the insurance cover provided by a P&I club.Limit of liability for loss or damage to goods carried by vessels had ben governed by international conventions issued for this purpose.

11.1   RISKS COVERED

The clubs offer protection and indemnity covers for a list of risks, including but not limited to

1. illness, injury, and loss of life (seamen);
2. repatriation;
3. personal effects;
4. illness, injury, and loss of life (persons other than seamen and passengers);

5. stowaways, refugees, or persons rescued at sea;
6. cargo liability;
7. collision with other ships;
8. damage to property (including fixed and/or floating objects);
9. wreck removal;
10. quarantine expenses;
11. towage;
12. pollution risks;
13. fines; and
14. defense coverage for legal costs.

11.2 Limit of Liability

The member could limit the required amount to be indemnified in case of each accident or per year risks and for any of the listed risks that their trade would require to meet their expected liabilities or to comply with the requirements of the rules and regulations on the visited ports for loading or unloading. Members may opt for several different limits that apply for different risk

Premiums (calls) are calculated individually. It depends on the limit of liability purchased by the assured, the deductible amount, and the vessel's specification, type, trading pattern, and loss record.

11.3 Exclusions

Major exclusions to P&I coverage include:

- Other insurance: A P&I insurance claim may be rejected if a club manager thinks the risk should have been covered by other types of insurance that the shipowner should have obtained

- Mutuality: The shipowner is demanded to take sufficient steps to limit liability in order to protect the club, otherwise claims may be rejected. Shipowner limitation will depend on the international conventions that govern the incident.
- Moral hazard:Shipowner is required to issue a bill of lading as an evidence of receipt of goods.Claims fraudulent nondelivery of cargo, especially deliveries of cargo that do not require an original bill of lading, are usually not covered by P&I insurance
- Willful misconduct: This conduct is excluded in all types of insurance, therefore losses intended by the member or to which it "turned a blind eye," knowing they were likely to happen will fall within the exclusion.
- Public policy: Criminal liabilities used not to be covered as a matter of course; criminal liability was imposed only for intentional misconduct, and the requirement of fortuity generally included the coverage of criminal liability

11.4 Relationship with Marine Insurance

Marine insurers offer insurance coverage on measurable risks, that is, known sum insured for hull and machinery insurance for, and agreed value forcargo insurance . P&I clubs provide broader insurance for coverage, intermediate risks that marine insurers usually do not cover, such as third-party risks. These risks include a carrier's liability to a cargo owner for damage to cargo; a shipowner's liability after a collision; environmental pollution; and P&I war risks insurance, or legal liability due to acts of war affecting the ship.

Marine insurers are usually profit shareholding companies that charge customers a premium to cover ships and cargo subject to agreed trms and conditions .

In contrast, a P&I club is run as a nonprofit association, and the insurance is financed by calls. Club members contribute to the club's common risk pool according to the rules of the pooling agreement. If the risk pool cannot cover current claims, the club members will be asked to pay further calls. If the pool has a surplus, the club will ask for a lower call the following year or make a refund to members. This is the pure system of mutuiality.However,only shipowners with acceptable reputations are allowed to join P&I clubs, and any member who incurs reckless or avoidable losses attributable to the club may be asked to leave.

CHAPTER 12

INCOTERMS 2010 RULES

12.1 Introduction

The movement of goods from one place to another either in domestic or international trade require the use of trucks, vessels, railway, aircraft or by post for transportation .The trade in goods is usually carried subject to sale agreement between seller nad buyer. The sale contract or agreement need to stipulate the rights and obligations of each party for the sake of clarity and to avoid as much as possible any legal dispute that may arise between the contracting parties. In domestic trade the contract of sale will be subject to the provisions of the national law. In international cargo transit it is recommended to apply standard international terms to pre determine the rights and obligations as well as the party to borne the cost of services that accompany the process of preparation of goods for the transport. Services may include preparation and legalization of official documents necessary for the export of goods as required by the export or import countries.

International Commercial Terms (INCOTERMS) are issued by the International Chamber of Commerce (ICC) as a contribution to standardise and simplify international trading practices. The first edition of the terms was published by the ICC on 1936 and developed to match with the development of transport. The latest version was issued in 2010 which came to effect on 2011.

The 2010 rules had been educed to eleven instead of thirteen according to the earlier terms. The old rules DAF(Delivery at Frontier), DES(Delivery Ex Ship), DEQ(Delivery Ex Quay(Duty Paid) and DDU(Delivery Duty Unpaid) were replaced by the new two terms irrespective of mode of transport: DAT(Delivery At Terminal, and DAP (Delivery At Place).

The terms were classed in accordance with the mode of transport used for the carriage of goods as per the below table:

Group A Rules for any transport mode	Group B Rules for sea and inland waterway only
Ex Works (EXW)	Free Alongside Ship (FAS)
Free Carrier (FCA)	Free On Board (FOB)
Carriage Paid To (CPT)	Cost and Freight (CFR)
Carriage and Insurance Paid To (CIP)	Cost, Insurance, and Freight (CIF)
Delivered at Terminal (DAT)	
Delivered at Place (DAP)	
Delivered Duty Paid (DDP)	

Bulk cargoes (oil, coal, beans, and so forth) and noncontainerized goods, where the exporter can load the goods onto the vessel are recommended apply the rules for transport by sea or inland waterways. Moreover, it is more appropriate to use , the "any transport mode" for containerized cargo.

12.2 Rules and Obligations
12.2.1 Ex Works (EXW)

The seller has to fulfil his obligation to deliver when he/she made the goods available at their premises (i.e. works, factory, warehouse) and at the disposal of the buyer.

The seller also has to provide the commercial invoice or its equivalent electronic message in conformity with the contract of sale.

On the other hand , the buyer has to pay the cost as per the agreed contract of sale and obtain at his/her own risk and expense any document necessary for export and import licences. The buyer is to bear all risks of loss or damage to the goods from the time they had been placed at his disposal.

12.2.2   Free Carrier (FCA)

The seller arranges precarriage of the goods from his/her depot to a named place, which can be a terminal, transport hub or forwarder's warehouse. He/she has to make goods ready for export and handover the goods to the charge of the carrier named by the buyer at the named place or point. If the buyer instructs the seller to deliver the cargo to a person e.g. freight forwarder who is not a "carrier" ,the seller is deemed to have fulfilled his obligation to deliver the goods when they are in the custody of that person.

The important difference between FCA and EXW that where the named place is the seller's premises, then the later is responsible for loading the goods onto the land conveyance.

The buyer obligation is to pay the price of goods as provided in the contract of sale. He/she has obtain at his/her own expense the required import license or other official documents aas well as to contract for the carriage of goods from to the agreed points.

12.2.3   Carriage Paid To (CPT)

CPT means that the seller has to deliver the goods into the custody of the carrier and pays the freight for the carriage of the goods to the named destination. The risk of loss or damage to the goods, as well as any additional costs due to events occurring after the time the goods have been delivered to the carrier is transferred from seller to buyer.

Insurance cost will be borne by the buyer who has to obtain the appropriate insurance cover for the main carriage, starting from the point where the goods are taken in charge by the carrier.

12.2.4 Carriage Insurance Paid To (CIP)

CIP means that the seller has the same obligations as under CPT but with the addition that the seller has to procure cargo insurance to cover loss or damage to goods as per agreed terms and conditions. The buyer should note that under the (CIP) the seller is only required to obain insurance on minimum coverage unless agreed otherwise.

The seller has to deliver the goods into the custody of the carrier for transportation to the named place of destination on the date or within the period stipulated in the contract of sale.

12.2.5 Delivered at Terminal (DAT)

The seller is responsible to arrange the carriage and delivery of the goods, unloaded from the arriving conveyance at the named destination. The named terminal may be in a port , container yard/ terminal , a warehouse or transport hub.

Risk transfer from seller to buyer when the goods have been unloaded. Therefore, the seller has to arrange the insurance for the risks of loss or damge from the point of loading until the named place of unloading. The buyer may wish to arrange for the insurance from the end point to his/her premises.

THE MARINE INSURANCE HANDBOOK

The buyer is responsible for import clearance and any applicable local taxes or import duties.

12.2.6 Delivery at Place (DAP)

The seller is responsible for arranging carriage and for delivering the goods, ready for unloading from the arriving conveyance, at the named destination. The conveyance may be a vehicle or a ship. The main difference from DAT, that the seller is responsible for unloading.

Risk transfers from seller to buyer when the goods are available for unloading, which is at the buyer's risk.

12.2.7 Delivered Duty Paid (DDP)

The seller has the obligation to deliver the goods when they have been made available at the named place at the country of import. The seller has also to bear the risks, cost, fright charges, clearing them for import, and paying all applicable taxes and duties at place of destination.

While the EXW term represents the minimum obligation on the seller , the DDP represents the maximum.

The term may be used irrespective of the mode of transport whether a vehicle , an aircraft , a ship , railway or post.

Risk transfers from seller to buyer when the goods are made available to the buyer, ready for unloading from the arriving conveyance.

12.2.8 Free Alongside Ship (FAS)

The seller fulfils is obligation to deliver when placing the goods along side the ship on the quay or in lighters at the named port of shipment. That is , the buyers has to bear all costs and risks of loss or of damage to the goods from that ;oint.

This term requires the buyer to clear the goods for export. It can only be used for sea or inland waterway transport and in situations where the seller has direct acess to the vessel for loading. It is recommended for bulk and noncontainerised cargoes.

12.2.9   Free On Board (FOB)

The seller fulfils his obligation to deliver when the goods have been loaed onboard the vessel at the named port of shipment. Consequently, the buyer has to borne all costs and risks of loss or damage to the goods from that point.

The point of delivery was used to be when goods pass the "ship's rail" according to earlier versions of the terms. However, the term was updated to reflect modern movement and loading operations of goods and avoid the image of an imaginary line.

The term is recommended for situations where the seller has direct access to the vessel for loading (such as bulk or non-containerized goods)

12.2.10   Cost and Freight (CFR)

CFR term means that the seller must pay the costs and freight necessary to move the goods to the named named port of destination. The risk of loss or damage to goods and any additional cost due to occurrences after the delivery of goods onboard vessel is transferred from seller to buyer.

The term is recommended for cases where the seller has direct access to the vessel for loading. The term is mostly used for the carriage of bulk cargoes or noncontainerized goods.

12.2.11 Cost Insurance and Freight (CIF)

CIF means that the seller has the same obligations as under the CFR but with the addition to provide on his own cost a marine insurance covering all or damage to goods during the intended carriage. The buyer should note that the seller has only to provide minimum insurance coverage unless agreed otherwise.

This term can only be used for sea and inland waterway transport

Risk transfers from the seller to the buyer once goods have been loaded onboard (before the main carriage takes place).

CHAPTER 13

LETTERS OF CREDIT

Letters of credit (L/C) are documents issued and negotiated by banks on behalf of their customers to facilitate international trade of goods or services. They are described as conditional orders to pay to the bank account of seller or provier of services an amount fixed by the L/C upon submitting named official documents to support the payment. The main types of L/Cs are the commercial and standby letters of credit. Commercial L/Cs are the most common and are the major and most effect tool for the exchange of goods between international traders who are in most cases do not know each others. The standby L/C is described as a secondary payment method , that is , the issuing bank would only pay the agreed amount of money to the applicant's bank only when the latter fails to fulfil its obligation to pay.

13.1 Definition

A letter of credit is a document issued by banks to guarantee that a fixed amount of money would be paid to the beneficiary on complying with the conditions of the L/C and presentation of named documents to facilitate the payment.

Letters of credit are an international financial instrument that enables traders in different countries to exchange goods for money provided that certain conditions have been met and official legalized documents have been presented in return of agreed fees or commission. In the absence of such tool the international exchange of goods or services could not be performed. Therefore, the use of L/C by banks or the other financial institutions become an important feature of international trade.

The L/C issuing bank acts on behalf of the buyer and will ensure that all relative delivery conditions have been presented before making the payment. Accordingly, the international banking system is considere as an intermediary between exporters and importers (sellers and buyers). However, it is necessary to be aware that the banking system does not take any responsibility to investigate the quality of goods, authenticity of documents, or any other provision in the contract of sale. The bank is to use due diligence in examining the documents that presented by the seller.

Banks prefer to apply the rules promulgated by the International Chamber of Commerce, known as Uniform Customs and Practice for Documentary Credits (UCP).

The parties to the L/C are the sellers who are the supplier of good or provider of services called the "beneficiary." On the other hand, the "issuing bank" acts on behalf of the buyer who is a client to the bank, and sometimes an advising bank, of whom the beneficiary is a client. L/Cs are mostly issued as irrevocable document, that is, they cannot be amended or canceled without mutual consent of concerned parties.

13.2   Beneficiary

The beneficiary is the party to be paid a fixed amount of money on presentation of documents listed in the L/C conditions or any other documentary evidence required by the letter of credit. The L/C is a separate transaction from the contract on which it is based. Neither the issuing bank nor the advising or confirming bank is liable for performance or the subject matter of the underlying contract between the customers and beneficiary.

13.3   Issuing Bank

In accordance with the terms of the L/C the issuing bank becomes liable to pay to the advising or confirming bank on fulfillment of the contract obligations from the supplier or the provider.Consequently, the issuing bank will be entitled to be reimbursed from its customer/client. The main role of the issuing bank is to guarantee payment of L/C money upon ensuring that the presented documents do comply with the L/C requirements.

13.4   Advising Bank

An advising bank is usually located in a foreign country and mostly in the applicant's place of residence. Its main role is acting as a corresponding of the issuing bank to advise the beneficiary. Practically, the beneficiary would prefer to use a local bank to ensure that the letter of credit is valid and the advising bank would is responsible for presenting the documents to the issuing bank.It should be noted that if the issuing bank does not pay the beneficiary, the advising bank is not obligated to pay.

13.5   Confirming Bank

The role of the confirming bank is to act as a correspondent that confirms the letter of credit for the beneficiary. This bank is usually but not always the beneficiary's bank.

THE MARINE INSURANCE HANDBOOK

Subject to the request of the issuing bank, the correspondent becomes liable to ensure payment under the letter of credit. The confirming bank would only confirm the validity of the L/C after evaluating the issuing bank where the letter of credit originates. The confirming bank is mostly the advising bank.

13.6 Elements of a Letter of Credit

- Issuing bank undertakes to pay to applicant bank a fixed amount of money
- Payment is made on behalf of the buyer(applicant)
- Payment is conditional on presentation of namedlist of documents representing the supply of goods or services
- Payment is to be made within a predertmined period
- Supporting documents need to be in compliance with the conditions of the letter of credit.
- Documents to be provided at a specified place and within an agreed time

13.7 Documents That Can Be Presented for Payment

1. Bill of Lading or similar document as an evidence that goods described on the L/C is shipped on board or matching with the incoterms used in the L/C conditions
2. Invoice or packing list to prove the supplied goods to be in compliance with the L/C
3. Insurance certificate or policy or any other docuemts subject to the incoterms applicable to the L/C
4. Official documents for export or import including license, embassy legalization, certificate of origin, inspection certificate, or sanitary certificate
5. Test certificate for machineries if required by the L/C

13.8 Common Defects in Documents

Almost half of L/C drawings presented contain discrepancies. That is, an error or irregularity in the declared information that do not comply with the letter of credit. It should be noted that L/C requirements cannot be waived or altered by the issuing bank without the express consent of the concerned parties. The beneficiary needs to prepare and examine the required documents carefully before presenting them to the paying bank to avoid any delay in payment. Common errors or discrepancies found between the letter of credit and supporting documents include the following:

- Period or time limit of the L/CThe has expired prior to presentation of draft.
- The bill of lading that evidences delivery of goods do not comply with the given time limit to ship or not in accordance with the agreed incoterms.
- Invoice or packing list included information that are not authorized in the L/C
- The supplied documents included description of goods that is inconsistent with the L/C.
- Insurance polcy or certificate does not comply with the LC or contract of sale.
- Value of goods invoice as shown on the invoice is not equal to the draft amount.
- Place of loading and unloading destinationPorts are not as specified in the credit.
- A document that is required by the credit may not be presented.
- Documents may contain general descripancies in respect of volume, quality, weight and so forth.
- Documents are not listed as described in the credit. (Beneficiary information must be exact.)
- The invoice or statement need to be signed and/or stamped as stipulated in the letter of credit.

THE MARINE INSURANCE HANDBOOK

If the negotiating bank detects a discrepancy, a correction to the document may be allowed if it can be done within the L/C time limit and while remaining in the control of the bank. However, if time is not a factor, the exporter should request the negotiating bank to return the documents for correction.

But, if there is not enough time to make the required corrections, the exporter should request that the negotiating bank send the documents to the issuing bank on an approved basis or notify the issuing bank to waive the discrepancy.

13.9   Types of Letters of Credit
13.9.1   Sight

A sight L/C authorizes immediate payment to the seller on presentation of the required documents to the issuing bank. Payment is made on condition that all requirements of the L/C have been met.

13.9.2   Deferred payment

A letter of credit with deferred payment means that payment to the seller is not made on presentation of the list of required documents documents but at a later time defined in the letter of credit.

13.9.3   Acceptance

An acceptance credit is similar to deferred payment L/C and payment to the seller is made at a later time defined in the letter of credit but not on submitting the required documents.

However, the seller can request a discount from the banks that accepted the bill of exchange, or from another bank, and thus draw the amount of the bill minus the discount at any time after the documents have been submitted and accepted.

13.9.4 Negotiable Credit

Negotiable letter of credit obliges the issuing bank to pay to the beneficiary and/or any bank nominated by the beneficiary. Such documents are passed freely between parties as money. The negotiable L/C must include unconditional promise to pay either on demand or at a determined date.

The term" negotiable credit" is interpreted in different way between the different banks in the world.

13.10 Particular Types
13.10.1 Transferable L/C

Transferable letters of credit allow an intermediary to transfer the document to a supplier or provider of services. This type of L/C is well-adapted to the requirements and simple operations of international trade. They enable the intermediary to reduce the extent to which it uses its own funds to process business transactions.

13.10.2 Standby L/C

Standby letters of credit is a type of guarantee through the process of bank documents and could serve a different function than a commercial L/C. A bank will issue a standby L/C on behalf of a customer as an assurance that the performing party will fulfil their obligations.

The bank's obligation is to make payment on presentation of the L/C documents.

13.10.3 Revolving L/C

Under revolving L/C the buyer requests partial deliveries/ shipments of the ordered goods at specific intervals (contract delivery by installments). Payment can be made under the terms of a revolving letter of credit to cover the value of each consecutive delivery/shipment. The bank is normally liable for the total value of all agreed partial deliveries.

However, the second partial payment will be made after the settlement of the first installment , and so forth.

13.10.4 Red-Clause L/C

Subject to the terms of red-clause credit (letter of credit with advance payment), the seller can request an advance payment (defined in the terms and conditions of the letter of credit) from the corresponding bank. This advance is mainly intended to finance the manufacture or purchase of the goods or raw material to be delivered under the letter of credit. This advance payment is made against receipt and written undertaking from the seller to subsequently deliver the transportation documents before the expiry of the credit time period.

13.10.5 Green-Clause L/C

Different thn the red-clause letter of credit, under a green-clause L/C, the advance payment is normally madepaid not only against receipt of an additional document providing proof that the goods to be shipped have been warehoused.

13.11 L/C and Insurance Policy

An insurance policy or certificate is a requirement for payment of an L/C amount. It is most usual that banks declare shipments for insurance and may also specify the risks and conditions that are required to be the subjects of insurance.

It may happen that conflicts arise between banks and underwriters on the conditions required by the banks who could be named as coinsured in the policies/certificates. For example, banks may not accept the addition of a condition for deductible or excess. Moreover, they may also reject an insurance policy that includes certain conditions, such as an Institute Classification Clause or to add the ISM (International Safety Management) Endorsement certificate or similar conditions.

Although the Uniform Customs Rules and Practice for Documentary Credits do not object to such conditions, banks might be applying strictly the L/C conditions as agreed by the parties to the contract.

CHAPTER 14

FRAUD

Fraud is an illegal and unlawful act by persons or parties committed with intent to deceit and misrepresentation aiming to gain money or services or property. It is the human nature of greed that leads Fraudesters to such performance. Fraud may be said to be old and ancient as commerce itself with examples traced back to the Roman world.

14.1   What is Fraud:

There are various definitions of the term Fraud but without a universal legal definition for maritime or commerce fraud which are easier to recognize than to define.Fraud may be committed in all aspect of our daily life practices. However, our concer will be on international maritime and commercial fraud.

International trade transaction involves buyer, seller, shipowner, charterer, ship master, crew, insurer, banker, broker, and agent. Maritime fraud may be committd by one of these parties occurs when one of these parties to obtaining money or goods from another party to who he or she has undertaken specific trade, transport, and financial obligations or any other mean of communications.

Parties to maritime or commercial transactions are often located in various countries and are subject to different laws and jurisdictions. Therefore, the international trade will require their trade transactions to be made either by outside or foreign parties as brokers, agents or other intermediaries. Modern trade will facilitate such performance through the financial institutions without the need for any of the party's to the contract to meet or have a physical check on the documents or goods related to the contract.

International as well as domestic trade transactions rely on documents. In international shipping the bills of lading are the evidence of the change of title and the carriage of goods to the buyer. Bills of lading are issued by carriers, forwarders, ship agents or brokers contain an inherent weakness although being a key element of the intenational trade. It is important to note that bills of lading are the root for most of the maritime fraud.

14.2   Cargo and Document Fraud

Cargo and / or document fraud could be committed in different forms. The shipping industry witnessed many cases of the sale of cargoes that do not exist , the unlawful claim under letter of credit , or the misrepresentation of shipping documents mainly the relative bill of lading. Other forms could be described as cheating over quantity or quality of cargo as well as theft of part or all cargo carried on board the vessel. Seafares or mariners may be assisted by third parties on shore to facilitate this form of fraud to sell the stolen goods.

14.3   Examples: (1) Forged Bills of Lading

Modern printing and electronic technology gave a space to this type of fraud.The fraudsters may be able to produce a fake set of bills of lading that looks sufficiently genuine to be presented to the carrier and take delivery of the cargo in advance of the true receiver.

Fraud cases of this type showed that "insiders" either from the vessel or the agent's office offered assistance to perform their act. Fradester need key information on the cargo and receiver(s) to create the forged bill of lading and ensure that they can take delivery at the port of discharge.

In accordance with the applicable laws or international conventions of the carriage of good the carrier may be held liable for not fulfilling their obligation to deliver the goods and /or to take care and due diligenceas custodian of the goods.The receiver or cargo owner may seek indemnity from the carrier or their insurer but it is not clear who is the party to blame and compensate the victim.

14.4 (2) Use of Containers

Modern shipping and latest invention of carriage of good by the use of the various types of containers on board vessels to ports of discharge had benefitted and facilitagted the easy move of goods . However this type of shipping had also given rise to numerous opportunities of fraud in many ports of the world. Cargo may differ from the ordered and agreed description or type or weight.

It was witnessed at many ports of third world countries to discover upon opening their container to contain old spare parts instead of genuine and new parts, bags containing sand instead of ferilisers , ceramic kitchen ware instead of christal ware....etc. These examples are few of what is still happening in the shipping industry. Some ship operators or agents would insist that their bills of lading to include a statement" shippers' load ,stow and count" to avoid dispute in cases as quoted above. Similar to cases of fraudylant bills of lading the victim may not be able to recover from their insurers or the carrier. In certain cases the commercial attaché in the embassy of the exporter country may be called to attend to support in legal action against the suppliers but most cases had failed due to the fact that suppliers disappear without any valid address or contact information.

Other examples of this type include the following:

1. A cargo of fine glassware was replaced by cheap and less value wares.
2. A forty-foot box contained illegal immigrants in collaboration with "insiders"
3. Cases witnessed the smuggling of drugs hiden in containers.
4. Waste and rubbish material may stowed in the container to give the impression of a certain number of tons of weight, but the real goods which are paid for were never shipped.

The quoted examples are few and in all cases the carrier may be at risk of fines, legal charges, rejection of cargo, detention of the ship , disposal of goods , and extra carriage or port costs.

Traders are highly recommended to appoint well recognized survey agents at port of loading or at time of stuffing the containers. Surveyor's role is to attend at supplier's warehouse or port of loading to carry out a physical check to prove that goods description, quantity and quality are maching with the contract of sale.Such step will assist to minimize case of theft or change of goods or even the disappearance of the contracted cargo.

THE MARINE INSURANCE HANDBOOK

14.5   (3) The Ship "Salem"

A well known incident in the history of maritime fraud was the deliberate scuttling of the vessel "Salem." She was loaded with about 200,000 tons of crude oil purchased from Kuwait Oil Co.

"Salem" arrived at a South African port to pump its load in spite of the fact that South Africa was subject to UN embargo.

While the tanker was off the coast of Senegal she was delibertly flooded and abandoned by the crew who were all saved and found well dressed as photographed by a passing by vessel.

Investigations proved that the vessel was deliberately scuttled with illegal intent to obtain money from insurers of goods and vessel by misrepresentation of documents and fraudulent incident.

14.6(4) Cyberfraud

Cyber attacks are committed by IT professionals who are well computer educated. It is a modern and widely developing area of risk for all companies across all industries. Such attacks could target banks, financial institutions , travel agents , airlines as well as any sector that applies the computer informationtechnology in their business. Attackers or as called hackers will need information and knowledgeto commit to make a target believe that a transaction is genuine. The key element of cyber fraud is information theft and the successful hackers can facilitate the wholesale theft of vast amounts of confidential information to obtain illegally mmoney or other financial benefit.

Examples related to maritime industry include the following:

- Theft of information through the ntercepting and monitoring of communications to and from shipping agents to exploit a whole range of fraud and other crimes, from cargo-related matters to smuggling activities
- Attempts to divert payments of reight charges to a shipping company by circulating genuine-looking invoices, seeking to channel third-party payments to new banking details

14.6   Legal Overview

The consequences of any fraud action could be graded as criminal act in many world courts. However, an attempt to make a fraudulent insurance claim allows the insurer to reject the claim, while at the same time exposing the fraudester claimants to the risk of being prosecuted in criminal courts for their attempts to defraud the insurer.

But, on the other hand, if a person accuses another of fraud, and the claimed accusation is found to have been untrueand made carelessly without firm basis, this can lead to the claimant's facing a countersuit for defamation from the accused party.

CHAPTER 15

THE SHIPS

15.1 Designs and Structures
15.1.1 The Hull

Modern merchant ships have evolved from the all-purpose tramp steamer of yesteryear into a variety of designs and sizes, some adapted for specialized trades in respect to a commodity to be transported or ports to be served; others are built to be as commercially flexible as possible, with the capability of carrying a selection of cargoes between a multitude of ports.

As its simplest, a merchant ship is merely an elongated floating box made of welded (very occasionally riveted) steel frames and plates, in such a way that the resulting structure can safely transit oceans in most weather conditions, both carrying its payload and when it sails empty, such as when it is in ballast condition. The body of this structure—the hull—is divided into spaces for cargo; propulsion fuel bunkers; freshwater, ballast, propelling and auxiliary machinery; maneuvering and cargo-handling equipment; and living space for crew and passengers.

15.1.2 Machinery

In light of the increase in fuel oil costs during the early 1970s, ship machinery designs' emphasis in maritime propulsion shifted from speed to economy. A modest reduction in speed and daily distance covered results in substantial savings in the costs of voyage bunkers, even in older vessels. This emphasis on economical propulsion continues, with better and more fuel-efficient main engines produced, and even with wind assistance (a throwback to the last century) being revived in a limited capacity. The main two proven and commercially viable methods of propelling merchant ships are diesel engines and steam turbines.

15.1.3 Dimensions and Plans

Dimensions are of vital importance in ship designs. Ship dimensions will govern the ports a vessel can visit, the dues that will be paid, canals that can be transited, the sizes of items of cargo loaded, dry docks that can be utilized, cargo handling, and even the number of crew employed.

15.1.4 Plans

A modern merchant ship is likely to be equipped with around 250 plans covering its hull, machinery, and equipment, in addition to manufacturer's technical material on the care, operation, and maintenance of auxiliary items.

Plans normally clearly state the scale to which they have been drawn, with some of the larger ones usually to be found at the scale of 1/200, such as one centimeter measured on the plan representing 200 actual centimeters on the vessel.

15.1.5 Tonnage and Cubics

Merchant ship tonnages and the cubic capacities of cargo compartments are of vital importance to those involved in sea trading, for the earning potential of much seaborne commerce depends on these.

15.1.5.1 *Cubic Capacity*

A given amount of any commodity will occupy a certain space of cubic feet per metric ton, but the space required varies considerably between commodities. A ton of corn, for example, may be expected to occupy about fifty cubic feet of space, while heavier iron ore requires a far smaller volume, perhaps around fifteen cubic feet for the same weight.

Storage factors of commodities are normally described in cubic feet per metric ton, whereas a ship's cubic capacities are often quoted in cubic meters. General-cargo ships and some other vessel types will have two sets of cubic capacities, one described as grain cubic capacity and the other as bale cubic capacity. The former is used to assess the potential intake of bulk commodities, and the latter is used for such items as baled, palletized, or bagged goods.

15.1.5.2 *Tonnage*

Every merchant ship is required to be measured by its national authority or by agents acting on behalf of that authority, such as a classification society surveyor, and it is to be issued with a gross and a net registered tonnage. These are used in assessing the vessel for various dues and charges and for categorizing the ship throughout its trading life.

In 1994, the Convention on Tonnage Measurement as issued by the International Maritime Organization (IMO) came into force for all vessels, and such measurement conducted under the auspices of any flag will follow the same internationally applied rules.

15.1.6 Loading and Drafts

By international agreement, the navigable waters of the world are divided into load-line zones—geographical areas described as either tropical, summer, or winter. Some of these zones are permanently tropical; summer and winter are seasonal, altering at various times of the year as the weather changes. Tropical zones are considered the safest, and consequently, ships carrying cargoes in such areas are allowed to be more heavily laden and to be deeper in the water than if they were in summer or winter zones, the latter being judged the least safe and most prone to heavy weather.

Full details of load-line rules and regulations applied under the 1966 Load Line Convention and applicable to all seagoing vessels are included in a booklet published by the International Maritime Organization (IMO).

15.1.7 Draft Calculations

It is not an easy task to load a ship exactly to its marks, as the vessel will be unlikely to sink symmetrically, with the uneven distribution of weight aboard in the shape of cargo, fuel, and so forth all acting around the center of buoyancy. The difference between the draft marks is called "trim." Thus, a laden ship with a draft of twelve meters forward and thirteen meters aft is said to be "trimmed one meter by the stern," with a mean (average) draft in such a case of 12.5 meters.

Masters must make allowances in their calculations when loading in freshwater conditions (such as a river, alongside a canal wharf, or in a mixture of salt water and freshwater) or in brackish conditions, such as those that may be experienced in an estuary.

15.1.7.1 *Deadweight Scale*

Most capacity plans contain a deadweight scale, which can be linked to a diagram of a ship's side adjacent to midships, and this is of vital importance to the sea trader. By diligent use of this scale, a user can calculate deadweights and/or displacements against particular drafts, or vice versa.

The deadweight scale provides a vital link between the general arrangement and the capacity plans.

15.1.7.2 *Stability*
Another concern of the master is to ensure that the load and the ship are stable and will remain so during the voyage. Merchant ships are issued a stability book, produced by a naval architect and checked and verified by a classification society.

15.1.8 Classification and Surveys
Classification societies are independent, nonprofit bodies directed by committees of persons representing shipowners, shipbuilders, engine builders, and underwriters. They exist for the purpose of ensuring that ships are properly constructed and maintained in a seaworthy and safe condition, and to fulfill this function, they make rules governing vessel construction, and they arrange and carry out surveys during the building of ships and throughout the vessels' subsequent trading lives. They also conduct research into all forms of construction, efficiency, and safety of seagoing vessels, offshore equipment such as oil rigs, and offshore plants.

It is not mandatory for a shipowner to enter his or her vessel in a classification society and subject himself or herself to these controls, but in practice, it would otherwise be impossible to trade. Trading certificates that need to be produced at ports of call would not be forthcoming, and it is essential to be properly "classed" in order to obtain adequate and economical insurance coverage. Moreover, most charter parties stipulate that a vessel be of "highest class" of the classification society in which it is entered, such as 100A1 at Lloyd's Register, the British society.

The leading classification societies belong to the International Association of Classification Societies (IACS), a body that seeks to internationally represent the societies. The rules of the different societies vary in detail but are similar overall.

They include:

CLASS	NAME	WEBSITE
ABS	American Bureau of Shipping(ABS)	http://ww2.eagle.org
BV	Bureau Veritas	http://www.bureauveritas.com
CCS	China Classification Society(CCS)	http://www.ccs.org.cn/ccswzen/
CRS	Croatian Register of Shipping(CRS)	http://www.crs.hr
DNV GL	Det Norske Veritas Germanischer Lloyd(GL)	http://www.dnvgl.com
IRS	Indian Register of Shipping(IRS)	http://www.irclass.org
KR	Korean Register of Shipping	http://www.krs.co.kr
LR	Lloyd's Register	http://www.lr.org
NK	Nippon Kaiji Kyotas	http://www.classnk.or.jp
PRS	Polish Register of Shipping	http://www.prs.pl
RINA	Registro Italiano Navale	http://www.rina.org
RS	Russian Maritime Register of Shipping	http://www.rs-class.org/en/

15.1.9   Surveys

Throughout its life, a ship is subject to periodical surveys designed to maintain its hull, machinery, and equipment in good condition. Certificates are issued as proof that the surveys have been conducted and the vessel found satisfactory. These surveys can be divided into three groups: those of "flag," others of "class," and other "general" surveys.

Flag Surveys: These are surveys required by statute and are normally carried out by classification societies acting on behalf of national governments.

Class Surveys: All seagoing vessels built and/or maintained in accordance with Class Rules and Regulations are assigned a class status, which is conditional upon compliance in regard to hull and machinery.

General Surveys: These are surveys conducted by a variety of organizations for a variety of reasons. Among the most important are the following:

- **Condition Survey**: These surveys are sometimes requested and carried out by insurers to prove that the condition of the vessel is satisfactory before assuming risk.
- **Damage Surveys**: Should a ship be damaged, various bodies may wish to inspect both the damages sustained and the repairs thereto.
- **Deratization Exemption Survey**: Every six months, a representative of a convenient harbor authority where a ship happens to be trading is called to examine the vessel and to confirm that it remains free of rat infestation, whereupon a fresh exemption certificate is issued for a further six-month period.
- **Cargo Gear Survey**: This occurs when a ship is equipped with derricks or cranes; it is essential that

these and their ancillary equipment (ropes and tackle) be regularly surveyed and certified to prove they are safe to use.

Valid certificates are useful guides to prove the seaworthiness of the vessels concerned, but there is no substitute for an inspection of the ships and the hard-won reputations of reliable shipowners.

15.2 Types
15.2.1 General-Cargo Ship

Deep-sea general-cargo ships tend to be fairly small in comparison with some of today's maritime giants; most ships of this type are in the 15,000- to 25,000-ton deadweight category. These are regularly employed on scheduled routes, are normally sophisticated, being built and designed to custom-serve those operations, and are termed "cargo liners," while vessels plying the ocean seeking cargoes wherever they happen to be are called "tramp ships," although this term can equally apply to tankers or bulk carriers, or any ship employed on a "spot" basis, voyage by voyage.

General-cargo ships today are similar to their predecessors hundreds of years ago, with the ability to adapt in order to safely carry a variety of commodities. This process of adaptation is illustrated in the evolution of general-cargo ship design in the period since World War II, when the famous "liberty" ships were constructed in the United States.

As trade patterns continue to change, the decline of older "tween-deckers" is hastened by unalterable design. The irregular shapes of cargo compartments and small hatchways make difficult or impossible the stowage and handling of that important cargo of today—the container.

THE MARINE INSURANCE HANDBOOK

15.2.2 Utility General-Cargo Ships

The 1960s saw the introduction of what may be termed "utility tween-deckers." These were intended for the tramp market, fitted with economical main engines and electric winches, and designed to efficiently carry the prevailing cargoes of that period, such as bulk or bagged goods.

Utility tween-deckers are the workhorses of the general-cargo tramp market, able to dabble a little in all trades but masters of none, relying instead on their flexibility and good fortune to secure business wherever events take them.

15.2.3 Multipurpose Tween-Deckers

The multipurpose tween-deckers are today's all-purpose general-cargo ships, fitted like utility tween-decks and capable of efficiently transporting the majority of commodities likely to be encountered.

Multipurpose vessels are usually fitted with derricks or cranes, individually capable of lifting full containers as well as providing heavy-lift facilities. Many of these vessels are fitted with their own lashings for securing containers; without outside, shore-based assistance, they are said to be "container self-sustaining."

15.2.4 Refrigerated Ships

Refrigerated or reefer ships are specifically designed for cargoes that would deteriorate in ordinary hold temperatures and conditions, such as meat, fish, vegetables, fruit, and dairy products. They are not true general-cargo ships, having no bulk-cargo capabilities, but they are fitted with numerous insulated tween-decks and can, if necessary, be used for the carriage of nonrefrigerated goods like cars; bagged, baled, and palletized cargoes; and sometimes even the ubiquitous container on deck. These are useful facilities, as the reefer trades are seasonal, and in the off season, these ships must hunt around for alternative remunerative employment if they are not to lie idle. Cold air is used to keep the cargo spaces under refrigeration.

There are container ships that have the capability to carry refrigerated containers on deck and in semi-insulated holds.

Recent years have witnessed profound developments in reefer ship design. There have also been significant new markets developed that help to spread the seasonal usage of these ships, and there has been a considerable increase in the general size of these vessels. Future trends depend upon whether the present dividing line between palletized and containerized methods of transporting reefer cargoes holds firm or whether one or the other of these modes gains ascendancy.

15.2.5 Bulk Carriers

Bulk carriers range in size from small craft to ships of over 150,000 tons' deadweight capacity, and as their name implies, they are primarily intended for the carriage of bulk commodities such as grains, minerals, and fertilizers, although they can carry other cargoes such as lumber, containers, steel products, and machinery.

Bulk cargoes can vary considerably in their stowing properties (stowage factors), such as ore around twelve cubic feet per ton and bulk barley at around fifty-five. Bulk carriers may or may not be fitted with cargo-handling equipment. Some are fitted with self-loading and discharging equipment. However, modern, sophisticated equipment is currently available whereby a ship is able to load and/or discharge itself without shoreside assistance. This machinery is normally tailored to a particular commodity and trade route, and is thus rarely suitable for a tramp bulk carrier, but only for a vessel built for a specific, long-term trade, such as bulk cement or coal.

15.2.6 Specialized Bulk Carrier Types

Bulk carriers, other than utility general purpose ones, are used to convey a variety of commodities; they range from those constructed to efficiently carry heavy, dense materials, such as ore carriers, to others that are lightly and capaciously built with volume cargoes in mind, such as wood-chip carriers. In between these extremes are found various bulk carriers built to carry particular commodities in addition to bulk cargo, such as "car bulkers." Although the applications are virtually infinite, among these specialized ship types are the following categories:

Ore Carriers: These specialized ships for the carriage of mineral ores were built in the late 1950s and into the 1960s and are often committed to long-term employment (such as ten years or more) on particular trade routes.

A highly specialized method of transporting ore is to convert it into a semiliquid state and move it as a slurry in a ship, which in reality is half tanker and half bulk carrier, but this carriage is limited to particular trade routes equipped with the necessary shore appliances.

Loggers: This type of ship emerged in the late 1960s and 1970s of strongly built, well-geared, handily sized bulk carriers. They are able to switch into ores or other heavy cargoes such as cement, if required, or they concentrate on other commodities, including that which gave them their name: heavy loggers.

Cement Carriers: There are two basic methods of transporting cement by sea, in bags or in bulk. Nowadays, ordinary bulk carriers such as Panamax bulkers are used to transport bulk cement. The air pollution at loading ports is overcome by cutting small holes in the hatch covers and pumping cement through one of these holes while sucking out air and dust from another, the openings being made good to the owner's satisfaction following the completion of the loading operation. At the discharging berth, holds can be emptied by modern unloading appliances, whereby air pollution can be reduced, although at many bulk-cement discharge ports, grab discharge is permitted; discharge can also be deposited into a depot ship lying off the coastline.

Mother ships or depot ships are increasingly being used as discharge terminals and are capable of transporting bulk cement from ordinary bulk carriers alongside, storing and perhaps bagging the commodity onboard, and thereafter distributing it as required in dust-free conditions (either in bulk or bagged).

15.2.7 Lumber and Paper-Products Carriers

The carriage of heavy hardwood logs is mainly the province for "loggers," but the timber trade also covers soft wood and its by-products, paper goods such as newsprint, wood pulp, and wood chips. This type of bulk carrier is constructed in such a manner as to attain the highest possible volume intake of cargo, clear usable hold space, and open-hatch accessibility, always consistent with ship safety.

Paper products comprise newsprint, linerboard, and wood pulp/wood chips, and the demands of this specialized field have given rise to equally specialized ships.

15.2.8 Car Bulk Carriers

These were first constructed in the 1960s and have steadily evolved through to the present day, and these ships are still being constructed, despite severe and increased competition from pure car carriers (PCCs), specializing solely in this market. PCCs are specialized ships used to transport cars around the world. The largest are oceangoing vessels capable of carrying five thousand cars or more, while in certain areas, particularly in Europe and Japan, smaller, coastal PCCs act as feeder ships for transporting approximately one hundred motor vehicles at one time.

On older car bulkers, the vehicles are lifted on and off by derricks or by cranes, and these ships are known as lift on/lift off (LO/LO) types, while more modern vessels have side ports and/or trackways, providing roll on/roll off (RO/RO) facilities.

15.2.9 Container Ships

The introduction of containers as a method of transporting goods at sea has had a profound effect on ship design over the last twenty years. Accordingly, most modern dry-cargo vessels are capable of carrying containers in addition to their main intended cargoes, and many specialized ships are today constructed with the intended facility of coping with two or more commodities, one of which seems inevitably to be the ubiquitous box.

Containers come in several regular sizes based on specifications laid down by the International Standard Organization (ISO). The two sizes most widely used in the marine field are TEU (twenty-foot equivalent unit) and FEU (forty-foot equivalent Unit).

The weight of a standard empty TEU is approximately two tons, and strongly built boxes are capable of sustaining loads of up to twenty tons. To this must be added the weight of spreaders used to lock onto and to raise a box, so a self-sustaining ship must have gear capable of safely lifting and moving loads of more than twenty tons—and double this when FEUs are involved.

15.2.10 Reefer Containers

These are specially fitted with internal motors, which keep in good condition the frozen goods and commodities that need to be maintained at specific temperatures. Modern container ships are fitted with reefer points to which refrigerated boxes can be connected and can operate via a ship's auxiliary generators.

15.2.11 Feeder Container Ships

It is uneconomical for large, oceangoing container ships to call at a multitude of smaller berths where a few of the containers onboard are destined. Also, the very size of such deep-sea vessels precludes their entry to many ports. Consequently, it is usual for one extensive container terminal to serve a general area with smaller feeder ships running between that terminal and local berths, moving incoming boxes to their eventual destinations and fetching outbound units back to the terminal.

15.2.12 Barge Carrying Vessels

Barges (or lighters) can be readily compared with containers. They are self-contained, while the principle of being loaded/discharged at places of origin/destination of their cargoes (and their transportation for many hundreds of ocean miles by a deep, seagoing mother ship) are all very similar.

The capacity of a barge is much greater than that of a container, and these larger, floating units lend themselves to the carriage of large unit cargoes, either volume or bulk.

THE MARINE INSURANCE HANDBOOK

15.2.13 Ro/Ro Ships

In recent years, vessels on which it is possible to drive cargo aboard (roll-on/roll-off) have evolved far beyond the popular ferry concept of small vessels linking nearby ports and offering merely scheduled sailing for passengers and a few vehicles. Now the spectrum ranges from large, high-speed, and capacious passenger/car ferries through to versatile, oceangoing RO/RO vessels capable of conveying a variety of commodities as trade dictates.

The concept of RO/RO ships being suitable only for short-sea service has altered radically over the last decade. In fact, for areas of the globe that possess limited port facilities, the RO/RO ship with its self-sustaining ability to load and discharge itself provides an ideal mode of transport.

15.2.14 Ferries

A modern ferry is often custom-built to serve a particular route, fitting comfortably into available berths with the maximum cargo/passenger intake capacity the trade will bear. Extensive terminals at either end of each route are often required, in order to handle the traffic and the documentation created, as well as to provide the modern facilities expected by the present-day traveling public and the authorities concerned. With the prospect of increased leisure time at the disposal of a growing number of people, coupled with their desire to remain mobile and to retain their personal automobiles it is highly expected that the car-ferry trade will grow and will be an attractive proposition for a number of shipping organizations that have specialized in this trade.

15.2.15 Crude Oil and Products Tankers

The largest tankers (and indeed the largest vessels in the world) are those concerned with the carriage of crude oil.

This commodity forms the greatest portion of the seaborne liquids market.

Tankers principally involved in the carriage of crude oil and its derivatives have steadily grown in size, until the very largest are presently around a half-million tons' deadweight; enormous ships limited by their vast dimensions to just a few trade routes. There are certain predominant tanker size ranges:

1. Ultra large crude carrier (ULCC): 300,000–550,000 tons' deadweight
2. Very large crude carrier (VLCC): 200,000–300,000 tons' deadweight
3. Medium crude carrier: around 70,000–130,000 tons' deadweight
4. Product carriers: 26,000–40,000 tons' deadweight

Tankers built primarily for the carriage of crude oil are capable of safely transporting other commodities, and with no specific preparation other than normal tank cleaning, these vessels can carry dirty (or black) products like heavy fuel oils, perhaps separating more than one grade; they can also carry other products of the oil-refining industry, such as carbon black (a dense powder with liquid characteristics).

Crude carriers' tanks can be cleaned sufficiently to allow certain ships to join product tankers carrying the clean products of refining industry, such as gasoline, naphtha, aviation fuel, diesel oil, gas oil, and such that need careful handling and the avoidance of contamination of any kind.

Tankers of around thirty thousand tons of deadweight are currently the main size used for the distribution of products from refineries to consumers, but with the development of new refineries in oil producing areas, the optimum size of such vessels are set to increase to around one hundred thousand tons of deadweight on certain trade routes.

Cargo Handling: Cargo is loaded by shore-based facilities, but discharging is performed by a vessel's own high-capacity main centrifugal pump operating at speed. Larger ships naturally have a greater pumping capacity, and as a result, most tankers of all sizes are usually able to discharge themselves within one day, provided that their pumps can maintain the standard minimum pressure of one hundred pounds per square inch at ships' rails as the cargo leaves the vessel.

15.2.16   The Combination Carrier

This is a group of ships designed and constructed with the facility of carrying oil and/or bulk cargo. These vessels can be subdivided into OBOs (ore/bulk/oil carriers), PROBOs (products/ore/bulk/oil carriers), and O/Os (ore/oil carriers). These provide their operators with the flexibility of transferring from the dry bulk to the liquid markets voyage by voyage or by prevailing freight.

15.2.17   Gas Carriers

Seaborne gas comprises natural and petroleum gases, each commodity necessitating specialized transportation to move it in its liquid state. The technical evolution has matched availability and demand for these products, leading to the creation and development of sophisticated liquid natural gas (LNG) and liquid petroleum gas (LPG) carriers.

LPG: Liquid petroleum gases, including butane and propane, are by-products of the oil industry; such cargoes emanate from oil installations for distribution. The carriage of these commodities can be 1) at ambient surrounding temperature under pressure; 2) in insulated tanks at liquefaction temperature but at atmospheric pressure; or 3) in a combination of liquefaction temperature under pressure. The latter usually applies today.

There is a high degree of danger associated with the carriage and handling of petroleum gas: ships involved in such transportation are fairly bristling with safety devices to supplement tank-design features.

LNG: Liquid natural gases, principally ethane and methane, cannot be liquefied by pressure alone, so they are carried at extremely low temperatures (ethane at -104°C, and methane at -176°C) and at atmospheric pressure.

15.2.18   Passenger Ships

Marine passenger carriage, other than short-sea craft, is today confined virtually to cruise liners, with only very few scheduled deep-sea passenger runs available worldwide. Suitable vessels are seasonally employed as "pilgrim ships," ferrying Muslim pilgrims to and from Saudi Arabia. In addition, there are various vessels serving as "floating hotels" in static capacities in certain parts of the world, but regarding oceangoing passenger ships, it is those vessels engaged with the holiday trades that hold our attention.

Cruise Ships: This type of ship is capable of a high passenger intake consistent with comfort and quality, utmost reliability to maintain demanding cruising schedules, and a reputation for the safety and enjoyment of those traveling onboard. Although the financial returns of this most sophisticated of trades are attractive, the vessels involved are of necessity extremely expensive, both to build and to operate, so that desirable objectives must constantly be aligned with economy of operation. Accordingly, in the typical modern cruise ship, much design work has concentrated upon operating economies, particularly regarding fuel consumption and manpower levels, as well as the important factor of appropriate weight distribution.

Another important facility of a cruise ship is its ability to berth and unberth unaided where necessary, with only limited assistance from tugs.

15.2.19 Livestock Carriers

The nonhuman deep-sea transporter or livestock carrier is a class of merchant ships capable of division between vessels designed for sheep and those for larger animals—primarily cattle. They are also suitable for horses, buffalo, and camels. There are approximately one hundred specialized livestock carriers at sea today; nearly all are the result of converting existing vessels to their present role. General-cargo ships, RO/RO vessels, and even a severely fire-damaged cruise ship have all been converted in the past.

Livestock vessels must be equipped with spacious carrying pens, comfortable, nonslip floors and ramps, enclosed areas that are well-lit and ventilated, and fitted with efficient and adequate means of feeding and watering the animals and for removing urine and dung. Extra accommodation is provided for stock handlers, and in some cases, veterinary surgeons are carried onboard.

Sheep Carriers: Sheep carriers are the large vessels of the deep-sea livestock market, most serving the high-volume trade between Australia and the Arab countries. With a large number of animals onboard (more than one hundred thousand is usual), the ships must consider fresh water and fodder consumption quantities as well as extra accommodation, over and above normal crew members, for those entrusted with the care of the sheep (the drovers and possibly a veterinary surgeon).

Cattle Carriers: Cargo sizes of cattle involve far fewer numbers than those of sheep, and this is reflected in the relatively small dimensions of vessels serving this trade. As with the sheep carriers, many cattle carriers are the result of conversion of existing ships, but this section of livestock carriers includes several custom-built vessels.

Cattle cargoes are centered on the trade between Europe (particularly Ireland) to North Africa and between Australia and the Far East.

CHAPTER 16

CARGOES

The variety of goods carried by sea is enormous, and along with relative quantities and modes of transport, it presents an ever-changing scene. Some commodities were forming a major factor in seaborne commerce half a century ago have lost significance, while others, like gasses, once thought virtually impossible to carry at sea, are now of considerable maritime importance. Recent years, moreover, have seen intense development in transportation systems, whereby packaged goods, perhaps in containers or in pallets, can be moved from one mode of transport to another without costly and time-consuming transfer expenses. The maritime industry has played its full part in this cargo-handling revolution, in the same way that railways, road transport, and canal systems have been required to adapt.

The different types of goods/commodities can be categorized as follows:

16.1   Wheeled and Heavy Units

Recent years have witnessed the development of seaborne carriage of wheeled and heavy goods from minor to major importance. Highly sophisticated vessels are currently employed in this maritime sector, and today's trader has the opportunity

243

of contacting and selecting competitive specialist carriers to assess and advise on the best methods of moving valuable goods and equipment.

16.1.1 Wheeled Units

This sophisticated trade can be divided into two distinct parts: that in which the wheeled units contain cargo, and that in which the wheeled units are themselves the cargo.

Wheeled units containing cargo include trucks towing TEUs or FEUs and trailers; they drive aboard purpose-built ships equipped with suitable stern and/or bow ramps and decks.

Wheeled units as cargo include bulldozers, agricultural and road-making equipment, buses, trucks, and cars of various sizes and weights.

16.1.2 Heavy Goods

Heavy goods include petrochemical machinery or entire desalination plants, electrical transformers, oil rigs, or similar units weighing over fifty tons per unit.

A new breed of ships has evolved to cater to the demand to carry heavy goods; these are termed "heavy-lift ships."

16.2 Grain Goods

As a seaborne commodity, grains can be said to comprise wheat, corn, barley, oats, rice, sorghums, soybeans, pulses, oil-seeds, and by-products of all these.

Whether transported in bulk or in bags, grains are liable to heat and/or sweat, especially if damp, when they may germinate or rot, therefore requiring careful preloading inspection, carriage, and ventilation. Because of these risks, grains should not be loaded or discharged if unprotected in inclement weather.

Carriage Regulation: Various regulations for the safe carriage of grain and its derivatives at sea resulted from the Safety of Life at Sea International Conferences of 1960 and 1974, known as SOLAS, which generated detailed rules for its transportation in a variety of sea vessels.

The main exporters of grains are the United States, Canada, Argentina, Uruguay, Brazil, Australia, New Zealand, Thailand, Burma, and the European countries.

Major importers of grains include Russia, Bangladesh, Japan, South Korea, China, Taiwan, Middle East countries, and East Africa.

16.2.1 Bagged Grain

Certain ports and infrastructures are not equipped to handle grain in bulk, in which case the cargo must be carried in bags throughout the loading operation, seaborne carriage, discharge, and distribution process.

Bagged grain is more laborious to handle than bulk, and more time-consuming still to stow. However, grain in bags remains an essential and major part of seaborne trade and will remain so as long as such cargoes need to be directed to poorer regions of the world whose people are unable to equip themselves with sophisticated equipment and that, in any case, have inadequate onward-transport facilities from their ports of discharge.

A further consideration with bagged cargo is the liability of damage to sacks during their handling, and thus the loss of valuable cargo through spillage, together with the risk of pilferage through the stealing of sacks, and of their miscounting at either or both of the loading and discharge ports.

16.2.2 Grains, Oilseeds, and Pulses

Whatever the methods of carriage and the problems inherent in the trade, the movement of grains comprises a considerable and versatile part of seaborne commerce.

In addition to those listed above, flour is a major commodity, as it is the ground product of grain, usually of wheat. Another important cargo, bran, is formed from the husks of grains separated from flour during the milling process. Meals are the result of grains being ground less finely than when producing flour, while the term "feed grain" applies to low-quality but still-valuable grain or grain by-products used in the feeding of animals and poultry.

Oilseed is another product of the grain family that is produced from a variety of plants. It is normally crushed prior to shipment and/or mechanically treated by a solvent process to remove valuable oils, which include sunflower seed, rapeseed, mustard seed, linseed, and lupinseed.

Seeds in bulk form are a dangerous cargo, being particularly prone to shifting at sea. It is also possible to "drown" in a hold of such a commodity. For these reasons, adequate securing of seed cargoes in vessels that are not self-trimming is vital, while seamen and shore labor must exercise caution when engaged in associated cargo work.

Pellets are manufactured from grain or seeds themselves or from residues produced in the milling process. If pellets are loaded at high temperatures or with excessive moisture contents, or if they are adversely influenced by climatic changes during the voyage, the cargo can overheat and/or sweat.

Barley: This is a generally light-stowing grain exported extensively in bulk and in bags from Canada, the EEC, and Australasia, and it is used in malt-making, bread, and cattle food as well as brewing and distilling. It is imported in large quantities into the Red Sea and Arabian Gulf countries in bag form.

Corn: This is also known as Indian corn and is widely grown in Southern Africa, the Far East, South America, and the United States. Corn is particularly liable to heat and sweat, especially as a result of poor handling.

Durra: This is a kind of millet much cultivated in Asia and in Africa as a substitute for rice; it is moved in bags over relatively short sea distances.

Pulses: This is a general name for certain food plants, such as peas, beans, and lentils, grown throughout the world, and all are capable of being processed for oils, expellers, pellets, and cakes.

Rice: Rice is the principal food of half the world's population, widely cultivated in Asia. Major exporters are Thailand and Burma, who export it mainly in bags; it is also shipped in bulk from the United States and Australia.

Rice is particularly prone to heat and sweating, thus requiring better-than-average ventilation, and when in bagged form, it requires adequate mats and dunnage to keep the bags from touching the sides of ships' decks. Some charterers/receivers insist that bagged rice be carried in electrically or mechanically ventilated vessels.

Wet rice is vulnerable to rot, excessive heat, strong odor, and dangerous swelling.

Sesame: This is a valuable plant seed, widely grown in India and other Asian countries and Central America, and it is exported in bags.

Wheat: Wheat is a heavy-stowing corn grass that provides the most important bread food of the world and is exported in huge quantities from Canada, the United States, and Australia, usually in bulk but occasionally in bags.

16.3   The Agricultural Products Family

The main agricultural products that comprise a large and valuable sector of seaborne trading include the following:

Cocoa: The kernels of the tropical cocoa plant, when ground to a powder, form the basis of cocoa and chocolate. Traditionally, cocoa has been shipped in bags from its main producer, Brazil, but bagged cocoa is increasingly being containerized. Great care must be taken in its handling, as it is apt to heat and sweat, and is particularly prone to mildew if wet.

The carriage of bagged cocoa is mainly by ventilated containers; an alternative is for it to be palletized on flat containers that are then wheeled into place on vehicle decks of RO/RO ships.

Coffee: When ground and roasted, the seeds of berries of this evergreen shrub, the coffee beans, form a popular worldwide drink and food flavoring. Shipped from various places, but especially from Central and South America, usually in bags, the beans taint easily and are liable to absorb moisture and to ferment, heat, and sweat. Good ventilation is essential, and most ships carrying this cargo will today be required to be fitted with mechanical or electrical ventilation.

Cotton: Cotton is a soft, downy substance resembling fine wool from the pods of the cotton plant, a flowering shrub grown annually from seed. Cotton is widely cultivated in subtropical areas, particularly in India, Egypt, Sudan, China, Australia, and the United States. Cotton is transported in bales to manufacturer areas. Bales vary in the way cotton is pressed together in certain compressing methods to reduce the required stowage space.

Sugar: Seaborne sugar comes mainly from the raw products of sugar cane grown in tropical climates. It is shipped usually in bulk but sometimes in bags. It is sometimes shipped as bagged, refined (the term for white) sugar and occasionally from either raw sugar obtained from the sugar beet plant grown in cooler regions or in the form of sugar beet pulp pellets that are normally carried in bulk. Certain countries lack either the shoreside equipment and/or the infrastructure to receive sugar in this manner and can handle only raw sugar in bags.

The carriage of white, refined sugar in bulk is rare because of the likelihood of contamination and perhaps of infestation. Consequently, nearly all such shipments are in bagged forms in fifty-kilogram units, which has been a convenient handling size.

When at sea, ventilation should be restricted, as excess air causes sugar to soften. Shortage of ventilation may create the buildup of carbon dioxide gas, so entry to cargo spaces should be exercised with care. Too much heat should be avoided, as, if overheated, sugar will harden, but if it is too cold, the sugar content diminishes. Ships' masters need to exercise skill if the cargo is to arrive in good condition.

Tea: The dried and prepared leaf of the tea plant shrub, used as a beverage and grown extensively in India, Sri Lanka, the

Far East, and East Africa, is shipped worldwide, usually in single or palletized tinfoil-lined plywood cases and in polythene-lined cardboard cartons.

If tea becomes damp, it loses aroma; it also taints easily and so should be stowed well away from odorous commodities.

Tobacco: The dried leaves of the plant are used for direct smoking or in the manufacture of cigarettes and cigars, for chewing, and in snuff. It is exported principally from southeast Africa and from the eastern United States in bales and cases.

The stowage factor of tobacco varies widely, depending upon variations in the weight of dried leaves and on the method of packing. If excess moisture is present in the cargo compartments, it leads to mildew, and tobacco is liable to sweat, to overheat, and both to taint other goods and to be affected by odors itself. Excessive ventilation reduces the flavor, but adequate air supply is necessary. Accordingly, ships with efficient air-exchange systems are preferred.

16.4 The Timber Family

The seaborne carriage of timber and its by-products (generally termed "forest products") encompasses hardwood and softwood logs, sawn lumber, wooden products (such as railway sleepers), by-products (such as plywood), pulpwood, wood pulp and wood chips, and paper products. Each in its own way demands specialized handling in sophisticated ships.

General considerations when carrying timber on deck encompass stability of the vessel, security of the cargo (avoidance of its shifting at sea), excess on-deck and/or hatch covers, safe movement of crew around the vessel, and visibility from the navigation bridge. The secure and proper stowage of deck timber has the effect of increasing a vessel's freeboard, and because of this, timber carriers may be measured and allotted lumber load lines in addition to the usual load lines, those being painted in at midship and permitting somewhat deeper loading.

16.4.1 Logs

Logs can be defined as heavy pieces of trimmed timber—either round, hewn, or sawn. If hewn or sawn, they may also be referred to as "balks."

Hardwood logs are the products of deciduous or of evergreen trees and include ash, beech, birch, elm, and oak from temperate areas and a variety of tropically grown timber, prominent among them mahogany and teak.

Softwoods come mainly from the coniferous trees of the temperate and subarctic regions of the world. These trees provide the raw material for sawn timber, pulp and paper, fiberboard, chipboard, and plywood, and they may be shipped in a variety of ways, usually as full cargoes, whereas hardwoods are often carried as part cargoes as liner parcels.

16.4.2 Sawn Timber

Much of the sawn timber transported at sea comprises softwoods, and these are used for the major purposes of building (both joinery and construction) and for packaging. The highest quality of softwood is used for joinery and the lower grades for packaging. Care must be taken during carriage to avoid mold and fungus, which may cause discoloration and the eventual rotting of the wood.

The timber market has developed into length- and truck-packaged lumber that, once laid, has a profound effect on the type of vessel employed in the carriage of this commodity. Today, such vessels maximize cargo intake in their unobstructed box-type, square holds, with large hatch openings, being usually equipped with their own cargo-handling derricks or cranes. Thus, loading or discharging is speedily performed, and the vessels' configurations enable them to carry containers in addition or as an alternative to packaging lumber.

16.4.3 Timber By-Products:

By-products of timber include plywood (defined as having three or more layers of thin wood laid with grains crosswise and joined together under pressure by adhesive), chipboard/fiberboard, comprising compressed and glued wood chips and fibers, and block board, odd cuts of timber, squared off and lined by plywood.

16.4.4 Paper Products:

Paper products are highly valuable, and great care must be taken in their handling and carriage.

Newsprint: The most valuable of paper products carried in large quantities is newsprint. Today, there are specialized vessels to transport this product in rolls, fitted perhaps with sophisticated suction-head-clamp types of cargo gear, enabling the lifting and stowing of several rolls at once.

The rolls are usually loaded end-on, several tiers high. Single-deck vessels with box-type holds and wide hatchways are used. Rolls should be well protected and secured to prevent them from shifting and becoming misshapen at sea.

Linerboard: These are brown paper rolls used in packaging and carton manufacture, also known as Kraft paper. Kraft paper weighs around one ton for each meter of length. Unlike newsprint, linerboard is strong to permit stowage on its side as well as end-on.

Wastepaper: Used for recycling in the paper industry, wastepaper is occasionally moved in large quantities by sea in bales of varying dimensions, particularly to India. The stowage factor of baled wastepaper is around 85–135 cubic feet per ton, but, if the paper is mechanically pressed, it can stow somewhat less than this, perhaps around fifty to fifty-five cubic feet per ton.

16.5 The Coal Family

Coal is a mineralized fossil fuel, mined extensively throughout the world and widely utilized as a source of domestic and industrial power. As a seaborne commodity, it is nearly always carried in bulk and is of considerable importance, being shipped in large quantities from the Gulf Coast of the United States, the western coast of Canada, and from Australia, South Africa, Poland, and Russia.

Much of the seaborne trade in coals is confined to large bulk carriers; therefore, the shipping industry relies on economies of scale on certain well-established trade routes. Few of these vessels have their own cargo-handling gear; they rely instead on loading and discharging at modern, deepwater facilities fitted with sophisticated equipment.

Coal in bulk is a difficult and dangerous cargo to transport, with four major safety considerations:

1) Gas Explosion
2) Spontaneous combustion
3) Cargo shifting at sea
4) Corrosion of ships' holds

Stowage factors of coal vary, depending on:

a) The size of coal
b) Whether coal is wet or dry
c) Type of vessel
d) Trimming
e) Origin

16.6   The Fertilizer Family

Fertilizers constitute a commodity grouping of major importance to seaborne trade, being carried throughout the year around the world in bulk, in bagged, and in liquid condition.

The trade comprises three distinct movements—that of natural fertilizer directly from its sources to regions of use and, secondly, to industrial areas where the base commodity is mixed with other products into compound fertilizer, followed by the third movement: the onward distribution of the product to eventual destinations.

A great deal of fertilizer (especially in its natural state) is moved in bulk, but certain regions lack the sophisticated port facilities and/or infrastructure capable of handling such bulk commodities, and consequently, export to these areas must be bagged. Bagged fertilizer is invariably quite safe to carry, but the transportation of certain natural and compound fertilizers in bulk may cause corrosion or other carriage problems.

16.6.1   Natural Fertilizers

Limestone: Limestone (calcium) is utilized in a number of industrial processes as a crop dressing or as an element in the process of manufacturing a compound fertilizer (calcium nitrate).

THE MARINE INSURANCE HANDBOOK

Nitrate: Sodium nitrate is a natural salt and a major export of the western coast of South America as well as from Chile and Peru.

Phosphate: Phosphate is an important volume commodity, the world's largest exporter being Morocco, and it is exported in its natural rock condition in large quantities from the southeastern United States, North and West Africa, and the Red Sea.

Phosphate rocks consist largely of calcium phosphate, which is used as a raw material for phosphoric fertilizer and for all commercial phosphorous chemicals.

Potash: This is a fertilizer used particularly to enhance light, sandy soils, and the term "potash" refers to any material (natural or a by-product) containing the element potassium. Most seaborne potash take the form of carbonate—a salt—a harmless, granular substance, although concentrated potassium chloride is carried under its more usual name of muriate of potash (MOP).

Sulphur: Sulphur is a yellow, nonmetallic element (brimstone) found naturally around the world, especially in North America and in certain volcanic regions. It is nearly always shipped in bulk in its various forms. It can, unless kept dry, be most corrosive to steel cargo compartments and can be the cause of some horrific problems in this respect. Sulphur is classified as a dangerous cargo in the IMO Dangerous Goods Code, although small sulphur fires can be extinguished either by finely spraying with fresh water or by smothering the affected area with more sulphur.

16.6.2   Artificial Fertilizers

There are many combinations of natural fertilizer and other elements of varying strengths used to create a whole range of compound (artificial) fertilizers, which are moved either in bulk or in bags around the world. Most are harmless and safe to carry, especially in bags, but a few can be explosive and/or corrosive, given certain conditions.

The main artificial fertilizers are the following:

a) Ammonium nitrate (AN)
b) Ammonium sulphate
c) Basic slag
d) Monoammonium phosphate (MAP)
e) Urea

16.7   The Cement Family

The carriage of cement by sea has grown steadily in volume. It provides a major source of merchant-ship employment. The product can be divided into bagged and bulk, the latter being capable of subdivision into finished cement and clinker.

16.7.1   Bagged Cement

As with many products, certain regions lack both the infra-structure and the port facilities to handle bulk commodities, and as a result, there is demand in these areas for cement imports to be bagged perfectly in single, manageable sacks.

The sacks utilized are usually of the paper type in several ply strengths that, although requiring more handling than units grouped on pallets, are easier to shift by a surplus of labor and in the absence of forklift trucks and other mechanized assistance, as is often the case in developing regions. At the loading end, however, many cement factories employ sophisticated appara-tus, enabling speedy loading by the use of single or palletized sacks on ships adjacent to the works, although a careful check needs to be made of hatch-opening sizes and of tween-deck clearances to ensure that the loading apparatus, forklift trucks, and any pallets themselves will fit into available spaces.

In addition to the loaded cement bags, a quantity of empty bags—usually around 3 percent of the number filled—are usually included by shippers to replace paper bags split open during discharge handling.

Jumbo, or big, bags made by polypropylene or PVC coated with polyester are a modern alternative to carrying cement in paper sacks; each bag has around one to one and one-half tons of capacity. The latest generation of heavy-duty, PVC-coated polyester jumbo bags are virtually climate-proof, can be utilized for storage purposes, and are reusable for up to several years and for many trips.

Additionally, cement in conventional paper sacks may be palletized, shrink-wrapped, in units of between one and one-half to two and one-half tons each, providing facilities exist at each end to maneuver and handle such cargo.

16.7.2   Clinker

This refers to bulk, partially fused, and unground cement in powder and lump form, prior to the addition of the setting agent gypsum. The absence of this setting agent means that handling in nondry conditions is not so critical, and loading/discharging can take place in adverse weather conditions if need be.

Just like finished cement, clinker can be extremely dusty and is subject to shore-based antipollution regulations.

16.7.3   Bulk Cement

Powdered cement in bulk is fluid enough to be pumped, and as a result, there exist cement tankers that have tanks rather than holds and rely on pneumatic pumps to discharge their cargoes.

Bulk cement can be quite readily transported in conventional bulk carriers, although cargo handling in these cases can be handled by one or more of a variety of methods. The simplest is to use grabs fitted either to shoreside apparatus or to the vessel's own gear for both loading and discharging. The problem with such a system is the amount of dust created. Consequently, some bulkers are loaded by pneumatic means, small holes being cut into the closed hatch cover of cargo compartments and pipelines connected to each—one or more through which to load cement, and one or more others to extract dust and air from the compartment. A further alternative is to discharge into the mother ship anchored offshore, where atmospheric pollution will be less obnoxious to the local environment.

Bulk cement is a perfectly feasible cargo for conventional bulk carriers, although it is important that before loading cargo, compartments are scrupulously clean and odor-free.

16.8 The Chemical Family

Solid chemicals and plastics, although comprising a small sector of seaborne commodities, are nevertheless becoming increasingly important to maritime trade.

Most solid chemicals are closely allied to the minerals from which they are formed. A few others are treated more as separate seaborne commodities. Among them are the following:

16.8.1 The Sodium Family

Caustic soda, also known as sodium hydroxide, is extremely corrosive (burning skin and eyes) and combustible (heating spontaneously if in contact with moisture or air). It can be formed from treating a solution of soda ash with a solution of lime to form caustic soda, mixed with calcium carbonate and separated by a filtration or decantation process. The remaining "pure" caustic soda is then shipped in drums as either a solid or in a solution. An important trade for this commodity is from Romania to China, where it may be used in a variety of industrial processes from petroleum refining to tanning and from soap manufacture to textiles.

Soda ash, a calcined soda (or sodium carbonate), is a white, powdery, anhydrous substance and is produced in two grades: light and dense (heavy). It has a wide range of uses, including glass and soap production, bleaching, paper and paint manufacture, dyeing, water softening, and metallurgy. Moved in bulk or in bags, depending on handling facilities, it forms an important seaborne cargo, particularly from Europe, the United States, and East Africa to the Far East.

16.9 Plastics

Most finished plastic goods are shipped carefully stowed in containers or on pallets with only a very small proportion loose for carriage as break-bulk general cargo. The base raw material for the plastic industry is synthetic resin fiber, whose properties vary widely or finished articles, depending upon both the raw materials used and their proportions. They are commonly transported in bags, which may be palletized to speed cargo handling and to ease stowage time. Depending on the place of origin, the pallets vary marginally in dimensions but usually comprise fifty bags of twenty-five kilograms each per pallet, resulting in a unit weight of about one and one-quarter to one and one-half tons.

16.10 The Reefer Family

Refrigerated goods, or reefer, involves the carriage of food goods on reefer ships in a specialized market mechanism. Over half of the seaborne reefer business is concerned with the carriage of vegetables, and trade is seasonal, relying upon the harvesting of crops around the world. Accordingly, owners of specialized ships engaged in this business may have little option but to seek alternative nonreefer employment in their trade's off season or to temporarily lie up.

Other than fruit and vegetables, however, the range of refrigerated goods carried at sea is considerable, including frozen fruit juice, flowers and bulbs; dairy products, meat, poultry and fish; pharmaceuticals; X-ray film, confectionary; furs; yeast; and even animal bones. Products are handled either as break-bulk, in pallets, or in refrigerated containers, depending on volume. They require specialized ship availability and infrastructure facilities at the loading/discharging places.

16.10.1 Cargo Handling

Break-bulk handling of delicate, refrigerated goods leads to a certain amount of cargo damage in excess of that experienced with palletized or containerized goods. Containerization is expensive, and not all products are worth the cost of adapting collection centers and ports to this mode of transportation. Consequently, palletization remains a popular method of moving such goods, as it is less expensive than containers, yet able to carry goods with less likelihood of damage sustained under the break-bulk alternative. Pallet sizes and weights vary, depending on the commodity and origin, a typical size being perhaps that for citrus fruits from Cyprus to the United Kingdom, with a length of 1 meter, a breadth of 1.2 meters and height of 1.91 meters, a weight of about one ton, and a stacking of only one tier.

16.10.2 Carriage Requirements

Ships built for reefer trading are expected to be capable of relatively high yet economical speed to assist with reliable marketing of the goods they carry; they incorporate improvements in insulation and ventilation technology to be energy efficient. General-purpose reefers must have the capability of providing wide temperature ranges, with the latest designs having a storage/carriage range in a constant, controlled environment between +12°C and -25°C, with the additional capability of completely changing cargo-compartment air contents up to around twenty-five to thirty times in every hour. The ability to simultaneously carry a number of cargoes at different temperatures is also important.

16.10.3 Freight

Although many reefer cargoes are loaded and discharged free of expense to the owners of the carrying vessel, much of this specialized trade is performed on the basis of liner terms, where the freight rate should include an allowance for cargo-handling expenses to be paid for by the owners, with the time so occupied being also the responsibility of the vessel's operators.

Freight may be paid in lump sum or, quite likely, as a rate per available cubic foot bale of cargo space in the vessel concerned.

16.11 Horticultural Goods

If the carriage of fruit and vegetables form the largest sector of the reefer trade, that of bananas is by far the most important commodity in terms of volume and that type of vessel's employment. Some reefers built with this one commodity in mind are specially constructed for lifetimes of service on particular banana-trade routes.

The main banana producers include the countries of Central and South America, the Caribbean, West Africa, and the

Philippines. The United States imports heavily from the Philippines and Central and South America; France and the United Kingdom have long-term contracts with the Caribbean and West African areas. Given the importance of this trade, an international banana association operates from Washington, DC, coordinating the plant's horticultural distribution against a background of overproduction and climatic difficulties.

In addition to bananas, other fruits regularly transported by reefer vessels include apples, pears, grapes, kiwifruit, and citrus fruits. All omit CO_2 gas, which must be strictly monitored and kept within the allowable limits, while as a general rule, the carriage of different fruits on the same circulation should be avoided.

Potatoes and onions comprise the lion's share of the seaborne vegetable market and are normally carried in bags. Other important perishable horticultural commodities carried on short sea routes include tomatoes, flowers, and bulbs, in a variety of transport modes, depending largely upon sea-passage time and on the volume the particular trade can sustain.

16.12 Meat, Poultry, and Fish

Nonliving organic cargoes such as these are generally hard-frozen prior to shipment, requiring low onboard temperatures of around -20°C to maintain this condition, although certain meats (such as Argentinian sides of beef) are carried in a chilled state at much higher temperatures. Market forces are gradually inducing trade-route alterations. It is felt that meat-consumption levels will be severely challenged by the increased popularity of fish and fish products, while mutton consumption in Arabian countries is already being offset by large imports of poultry, a major exporter of this latter product being Brazil.

Fish is very liable to taint other cargoes, so not only should it be stowed separately and hard-frozen (except for salted fish), the carrying compartments should be thoroughly cleansed and deodorized following its discharge. Fish products form a diverse market of great potential and one that is liable to expand considerably.

The stowage factors of meats vary widely, depending upon whether the product contains bones or is boneless; is in carcass form or is cut; and is in cartons or free. There are various ways of packing fish, depending as much on the traditions at the place of origin as on convenience to the shipper/carrier.

16.13   The Livestock and Animal Products Family
16.13.1   Livestock
In terms of numbers, the most important livestock trade is that from Australia to the Middle East, several vessels on this route being capable of carrying over one hundred thousand animals above the weather deck in tiers of specially constructed pens. Drovers (who care for the sheep) ensure they are regularly fed and watered, while a veterinary surgeon, carried aboard the larger ships, oversees animals affected by illness or injury. These personnel are signed on as crew members subject to the shipmaster's authority, and are fed and accommodated by the shipowner. The wages of these men and women, however, are the responsibility of the shippers/charterers, who also pay for repatriation expenses once the voyage is completed, whereas the cost of their food and accommodation is a matter for negotiation.

Smaller animals carried at sea are regulated by animal weight, ranging from twenty to 250 kg each, and are mainly exported from Australia, but also from New Zealand, South Africa, and South America. A far lesser numbers of pigs and goats are exported from areas such as Africa. Large beasts include cattle (250–6,690 kg) from Australia to subcontinents, and camels (800–1,300 kg) from Australia and around the African and Middle Eastern coasts. Large numbers of cattle and horses (400–7,700 kg) are carried on short sea routes around Europe, while, during certain religious occasions, copious numbers of sheep are shipped from local sources to the Red Sea ports of Saudi Arabia.

Strict regulations govern the safe and humane carriage of livestock from many countries, stipulating the size, construction material, and capacity of pens; deck height air changes per hour; lighting arrangements; fresh water and fodder storage and supply; cleaning of animal accommodations; sewage disposal; care of animals; and construction and angles of ramps/lifts for the boarding and disembarkation of animals. Standards of carriage in some countries leave much to be desired, and it is to be hoped that international regulations can be evolved and enforced worldwide in due course. Nevertheless, a carrier cannot be expected to have expert knowledge of the needs of a wide range of animals, and specialist overseers should be carried aboard with this responsibility, bills of lading being closed with "carrier not responsible for mortality."

16.13.2 Animal & Fish Products

Dairy goods: Not all dairy goods need the care of refrigerated transportation. Milk, for example, can be processed, powdered, or canned and carried more conventionally; powdered milk can be carried in bags on pallets in electrically ventilated holds.

Hides, Skins, and Furs: Animal hides comprise wet hides, dry hides, skins, furs, and wool. There are widely varied methods of packing, ranging from bales or bags, loose or palletized, to casks or barrels.

Wet hides are shipped either salted or pickled, in barrels, bales, or bags; they are occasionally loose. They will dry out on passage, and care must be taken to facilitate drainage into bilges and to keep them cool and provide adequate ventilation.

Great care should be taken when examining cargo's condition at the loading port, on which occasion the assistance of an experienced surveyor may need to be sought, when the true description of the cargo must be entered in the bills of lading.

Dry Hides: These are transported in various modes, but usually in bales (machine-pressed or ordinary), the stowage factor depending upon the packing method and on the moisture content of the hides/skins.

Furs: Furs are often extremely valuable, and care must be taken to avoid pilferage. Consequently, accurate tallying is essential. Additionally, furs create the same difficulties of carriage as do dry hides, except that with the most valuable of these goods, carriage in a controlled environment at around +2.0°C to +5.0°C with efficient ventilation is required.

Wool: Wool presented for loading in burlap/hessian-covered bales, may have been pressed (dumped) by a variety of methods or may have remained unpressed, thus covering a wide range of stowage factors, which depend also on whether the bales be stowed in a conventional manner or randomly stowed. The latter method takes up perhaps 15 percent more cargo space. They may also be strapped together for unitized handling. Additionally, they may be greasy or may have been cleaned prior to shipment, and as with other skins/hides, rust damage should be carefully avoided.

Wool is especially prone to spontaneous combustion; it is traditionally exported from New Zealand in utility containers.

Modern-density machinery may allow shippers to stow up to 120 bales in a TEU box.

Fish Meal: The most important fertilizer is a widespread, major import of Peru and Chile, manufactured from the residue of locally caught sea fish following the extraction of their oil. It may be shipped as powder in bags or in the form of bulk pellets, and care should be taken to check whether it has been treated with an antioxidant to suppress its tendency to overheat during passage. Untreated fish meal must be weathered for at least fourteen days prior to shipment, on which occasion the cargo temperature must not exceed 35°C, and its moisture content should not be more than 12 percent or its fat content also 12 percent of the cargo weight. Bulk, untreated fish meal may be carried only in temperate waters for voyages of a maximum of twenty-one days' duration, provided the cargo surface is thoroughly covered by plastic sheeting, forming an effective air barrier. Failing this, the carrying vessel must be equipped with a cargo-hold inert-gas system so as to keep the oxygen content below 2 percent of the cargo-space volume.

Because of the dangers inherent in the carriage of fish meal, both the IMO and local administrations have created regulations relating to cargo weathering, treatment by antioxidants, and moisture content.

16.14 The Liquid Family

Seaborne liquids range from drums of products such as bitumen capable of carriage in conventional tween-deck vessels, to parcels of delicate, edible oils transported in the specially coated and heated tanks of liquid-parcel tankers, to huge, homogenous cargoes of crude mineral oil carried in bulk in specialized giant ships.

16.14.1 Carriage Containers

It is sometimes found to be convenient to move small parcels of liquids in standard two-hundred-liter (forty-five-gallon) metal drums; they have the advantage of being easily transferable from the place of origin via a variety of transport modes to their destination without the need for sophisticated handling apparatus. Disadvantages include, however, the risk of damage (and therefore cargo leakage) to drums; loss of stowage space in rectangular cargo areas; restriction in the number of tier heights in cargo holds; and slow loading, stowage, and discharging. Modern attempts to speed the handling of drums include palletization and universal drum-cargo clamps, some capable of lifting together units of eight or so individual drums from wharf to stowage position, or vice versa.

16.14.2 Cargo Handling

As many liquids cool (vegetable oils), they will solidify into fats or become generally viscous and difficult to handle. For this reason, heating coils are fitted to some cargo compartments to maintain cargo temperatures and facilitate handling. Care must be taken to heat most products gently, to avoid the risk of scorching and damaging cargo. Furthermore, most liquid cargoes require the utmost cleanliness in their carriages to avoid contamination. Pumps and cargo lines must be clean and free from odor, every effort being made to avoid admixture of adjacent stowed liquid.

Today, many cargo tanks are coated with special paints that assist with cleanliness and reduce "clingage," the term given to describe the situation wherein remnants of liquid products adhere to tank sides following discharge, not only increasing cleaning work, but reducing the cargo quantity discharged ("out-turned"). Many cargoes are very valuable, and out-turn is carefully monitored.

A watch must also be kept to prevent smoking and open flames near liquid products, nearly all of which are flammable, some more so than others. Those products particularly hazardous and liable to explosion and burning can be identified if their flash point is below a temperature of 23°C; these, as a result, are subject to strict regulations.

Great care must also be taken to avoid pollution, especially when loading or discharging cargo or when cleaning tanks.

16.14.3   Density and Temperature

Liquids are similar in that they will fill a container of any shape into which they are placed. The space requirements of a given tonnage will vary, however, depending not only on the nature and density of the liquid substance but upon its temperature. So, unlike solid products, the volume requirements of which are unaffected or only marginally altered by contrasting temperatures, stowage factors are of little use in measuring the space requirements of liquid products. Instead, specific gravity or density factors are used, which can be defined as: "The ratio of a volume of a liquid substance at its actual temperature to the weight of an equal volume of pure water at a fixed temperature."

The specific gravity of pure water on which the system is based is taken to be 1.00—a density of approximately one thousand ounces per cubic foot. Salt water, on the other hand, is slightly heavier and is accorded a specific gravity of about 1.03. Thus, about 0.97 tons of fresh water equate to approximately one ton of salt water or, conversely, that a given quantity of salt water will be about 1.03 times heavier than the same quantity of fresh water.

Most oil tankers are filled only to 98 percent of total capacity to permit expansion during the voyage; the vessels' capacity plans usually have tables based on this percentage for ease of voyage and cargo calculations.

16.14.4 Cargo Measurement

To measure the weight of liquid in a container, it is first necessary to establish volume and temperature. For a ship, its liquid-cargo temperature can be found with the aid of cargo-compartment thermometers, volume being established by checking the distance from a fixed point on the vessel's deck to the surface of oil in the tank immediately beneath; this distance is known as "ullage." Each tank vessel carries aboard calibration tables, enabling allowance to be made for any trim or listing of the ship affecting this calculation, the adjusted ullage distance then being used in conjunction with a set of tables giving the volume of liquid in each cargo tank at various ullage scales. This establishes the actual volume of liquid in the tank concerned.

16.15 The Gas Family

Seaborne gas is carried in liquefied form and can be divided into liquid petroleum gas (LPG) and liquid natural gas (LNG).

Liquid petroleum gases comprise mixtures of petroleum hydrocarbons, consisting mainly of propane and butane as well as various "chemical gases" derived from the petroleum industry.

LPG and LNG can be transported at sea in a variety of ways:

a) Under pressure at ambient temperature
b) Fully refrigerated at temperatures between -30°C to -45°C, except ethylene, which has a boiling point around -104°C
c) Semirefrigerated under a combination of pressure and reduced temperature

LPG cargoes are handled in closed systems under a slight positive pressure or overpressure to prevent the ingress of air. For the loading operation, petroleum gases are liquefied by reducing their temperatures ashore sufficient for the product concerned. Most LPG tankers are able to reduce to and/or maintain temperatures at -50°C, any gas vaporizing during this operation being reliquefied by the ship's own liquefaction system. These low temperatures are maintained during transit, with the gas vaporizing during the voyage again being returned to its liquefied state via the ships' equipment before being returned to the cargo tanks.

During discharge of the liquefied gas, tank pressures reduce as the cargo liquid level lowers, and the constant pressure to assist discharge is maintained by the supply of gas from facilities ashore.

LNG is found naturally, but prior to transportation, its most dangerous impurities (such as sulphur and carbon dioxide) have been removed. By far, the major LNG seaborne gas is methane, with ethane, propane, and butane making up the balance. LNG is moved at or near its boiling point of -165°C around atmospheric pressure.

One of the particular features in the transportation of LNG is the use of cargo boil-off, gas vaporizing through heat leaking into the cargo tanks being utilized as fuel for steam turbines or potentially for diesel-powered propulsion.

16.16   Dangerous Goods

Under the auspices of the IMO, a Dangerous Goods Code has evolved. It encompasses recommendations as to stowage, carriage, packaging, documentation, and labeling of the most dangerous commodities. In many ports of the world, this code has been given legal enforcement and has been embodied into local laws and regulations.

The code classifies dangerous goods as follows:

Class 1: Explosives

Class 2: Gases: Compressed, liquefied or dissolved under pressure

Class 3: Inflammable liquids

Class 4a: Inflammable solids

Class 4b: Inflammable solids or substances liable to spontaneous combustion

Class 4c: Inflammable solids or substances that, in contact with water, emit inflammable gases

Class 5a: Oxidizing substances

Class 5b: Organic peroxides

Class 6a: Poisonous (toxic) substances

Class 6b: Infectious substances

Class 7: Radioactive substances

Class 8: Corrosives

Class 9: Miscellaneous dangerous substances

16.17 Nuclear Material

The gradual construction of nuclear-power facilities around the world has created a demand for the seaborne transportation of waste (or spent) radioactive fuel and, following its reprocessing, the further shipment of enriched material.

This is a specialized trade; usually, heavy and sophisticated containers are utilized to transport small amounts of radioactive material in equally sophisticated ships. The demand for shipment of spent and enriched material is rising, due to the increase in the use of nuclear power.

REFERENCES

CII Study Courses:
Principles of Reinsurance, Study Course 830
Practice of Reinsurance, Study Course 835
Marine Underwriting, Study course 190M/073

Clarke, Malcolm A. *International Carriage of Goods by Road: CMR.* (London, Stevens And Sons, 1982).

Goodacre, J. Kenneth. *Goodbye to the Memorandum.(London, Witherby & Co.,1988, 1ˢᵗ Edition)*

www.gov.uk/incoterms-international-commercial-terms

Hudson, N. G. and J. C. Allen. *The Institute Cargo Clause Handbook.London. Lloyd's of London Press LTD, LLP 1986)*

Ivamy, E. R. Hardy. *Chalmars' Marine Insurance Act, 1906 (9th ed.).(London, Butterworths, 1983)*

Packard, William V. *Sea-Trading (Cargo).Great Britain, Fairplay Publications Ltd,1985)*

Packard, William V. *Sea-Trading (The Ships, volume 1), Great Britain, Fairplay Publications Ltd, 1984)*

www.rhlg.com/Richard Hogg Lindley